ADV

Crazy Peace

"When I first met Linda, I felt as if I already knew her—she has one of those personalities that literally grabs you! I don't know, maybe it's because we were both from south Louisiana. In reading her book, *Crazy Peace*, I am amazed at how well she put her life experience in words and how we can all see ourselves in it somewhere.

"I highly recommend Linda's book as an encouragement and exhortation to press on in spite of difficulties and trials. I've seen how Jesus has used Linda in so many ways to personally touch the lives and hearts of so many with God's truth. Hope will spring up as you go through these chapters and you see that you can put your trust in the One who can do 'immeasurably more than we can ever ask or think.'"

—**KEITH THIBODEAUX,** executive director of *Ballet Magnificat!* and a former child actor who played Little Ricky in *I Love Lucy* and John Paul on the *Andy Griffith Show*

"In *Crazy Peace*, all of us can find many relatable moments. From the funny to the deeply serious, Linda Hurstell's true stories provide evidence of faith in action. The incredible results remind us once again—miracles still happen in the twenty-first century. We simply must open our eyes to see them. The nuggets of wisdom and insights inside this book sometimes take you by surprise, sharpening your mind, encouraging your spirit and warming your heart."

—**ANITA AGERS-BROOKS,** international speaker and award-winning and best-selling author of multiple titles, including *Getting Through What You Can't Get Over*

"Out of the richness of a lifetime of walking with God, Linda Hurstell has written a book that will make you laugh and cry, it will challenge and inspire you. This honest, vulnerable sharing of her many experiences demonstrates God's love and faithfulness. Linda invites the reader to partake of the *Crazy Peace* that can be theirs, even in times of chaos. This book will benefit every person who picks it up, opens it, and begins to read."

—**ROBIN GILMAN,** author of *Stress-Free Homeschooling*, speaker, wife, mother of ten

"I absolutely couldn't stop reading *Crazy Peace*. One chapter beckoned me to read the next and the next and the next. I'll admit it—as I read—it wasn't always a pretty picture. I giggled my way through some chapters and bawled my way through others. Linda has a rare gift for transforming ordinary life moments into the stuff of which miracles are made. Her perspective and intuitive nature make this book a grand read for those who are searching for God's fingerprint in a common life."

—**CAROL MCLEOD,** blogger, podcaster, Bible teacher, and best-selling author of *Rooms of a Mother's Heart, Vibrant, Significant* and other titles

"So often, we forget that God is in the midst of our everyday experiences, and when things become difficult, we sometimes ask 'where is God?' The stories in this book, *Crazy Peace,* remind us that the peace we have been promised by Jesus does seem a little crazy at times—yet it is always present and always comforting. These stories invite us to be sensitive to the presence of God in our own lives as we move along our earthly journey. The presence of God through His messengers and the Holy Spirit remind us that we are loved and cared for in every circumstance of this life. Linda Hurstell's personal stories show us how we can be thankful that He understands our needs, both small and large."

> —RICKEY L. HAYNES, District Superintendent, Mississippi Conference, The United Methodist Church

"As people of faith, our individual journey with Jesus is often best described as a series of occasions to walk with him along various paths. Linda Hurstell has captured these journeys in a cascading stream of vignettes. She communicates so vividly that the reader feels as if a beloved friend has shared details of her family in ways that reflect and reveal the compassion of God and the comforting presence of the Holy Spirit. Without being overbearing or condescending, Linda connects familiar scriptures with all-too-common experiences helping us all hear the calming words of assurance that make the desirable goal of peace possible.

Crazy Peace is a book that will find popularity among Sunday school classes, Christian book clubs, reading groups, and family gatherings, as well as a personal devotional resource for individuals. For mothers who may be struggling with a recent cancer diagnosis or for parents who are concerned about the effectiveness of their efforts to provide foundational spiritual lessons for their children, *Crazy Peace* offers instruction and inspiration."

—**JON E. MCCOY,** MDiv, PhD, Congregational Care Pastor, Christ United Methodist Church

"As one who seeks out everyday examples of how to overcome despair and land in hope, I feel deeply satisfied after reading *Crazy Peace*. I laughed out loud, cried and sighed, and now the identity center in my brain is nourished and equipped with examples of how to navigate loss, anxiety, shame, parenting and hearing from God. I have several inspiring and practical phrases running through my mind, such as *'live temporarily permanent and not permanently temporary.'*

"Here is the mentor, spiritual mom, or sister you are searching for. Author Linda Hurstell shows us how to be humble, realistic, direct, adventurous, resilient, courageous, grateful, able to shake off shame, secure in our humanity and secure in a relationship with the God of 'crazy peace' and intimate comfort."

—**LISA PINKHAM,** author of *Real Talk with God: How to Get Your Head Out of the Ditch of Despair* and Journey Group Facilitator with Deeper Walk International

"I finished reading Linda Hurstell's book, *Crazy Peace,* and found myself reading it again. I had gone on a journey with Linda where

I learned how she finds God in everyday life and the guidance and joy that happens when she recognizes it. I found myself reflecting on my own life and seeing events and circumstances in a different way. Wonderfully, I now look for God's presence in my life in both large and small instances, happy and tragic events happening to me, my family, friends, strangers, and the many children I encounter daily. Thanks, Linda!"

—**KATHY RIEDLINGER,** CEO/Head of School,
Lusher Charter School

"In *Crazy Peace* Linda Hurstell engages her readers by generously sharing stories from her life and interpreting them through deep personal faith. Scholars concluded long ago that religions offer their followers ultimate meanings for the mundane, joyful, and devastating events of their lives. In this utterly sincere book, we witness that process of seeking and finding ultimate meaning unfold in the life of a fully committed person of faith. By the way, this Christian can write."

—**MICHAEL A. COWAN,** Ph.D., Professor emeritus,
Institute for Ministry Loyola University

CRAZY
PEACE

TRUE STORIES
of GOD'S TOUCH *in*
EVERYDAY LIVES

LINDA HURSTELL

BROOKSTONE
PUBLISHING GROUP

This book is dedicated first to God
for giving me the desire and joy
to write about His crazy peace.

And then to my beloved Mackey,
our children and grandchildren.

*Now faith is the certainty of things hoped for,
a proof of things not seen.*

—HEBREWS 11:1

Contents

Introduction...1

SECTION 1: GOD'S CRAZY PEACE OF PROTECTION 5

    Chapter One: Angelic Incognito 7

    Chapter Two: Babysitting Betsy the Ballet Boa................17

    Chapter Three: Can You Hear Me Now? 28

    Chapter Four: Chinese Jewelry Heist 34

    Chapter Five: Crisis at the Gas Pump...............................42

    Chapter Six: Lawn Dart Drama 50

    Chapter Seven: Half Is Never Enough...............................56

    Chapter Eight: Olive Jar Bandit 63

    Chapter Nine: What's Next, Lord? I'm Ready 70

SECTION 2: GOD'S CRAZY PEACE OF PROVISION 79

    Chapter Ten: Chicken Pox and a Mini Print Dress...........81

    Chapter Eleven: Crawfish Hunter 92

    Chapter Twelve: Experiencing the Drama of God 100

    Chapter Thirteen: It's All Greek to Me 108

    Chapter Fourteen: Misplaced Lace 115

    Chapter Fifteen: Nutty Kind of Faith.............................123

    Chapter Sixteen: Sweet Aroma of the Savior...................131

    Chapter Seventeen: I'm Only Going in Blue 138

    Chapter Eighteen: Glass Deception..................................147

    Chapter Nineteen: Wrangling the Ginormous................154

SECTION 3: GOD'S CRAZY PEACE OF ASSURANCE 163

    Chapter Twenty: Birds, Trains, and Parking Spaces.........165

    Chapter Twenty-One: Forever Fingerprints of Fury........173

    Chapter Twenty-Two: His Voice, Your Story 181

    Chapter Twenty-Three: Nine-Year-Old Miracle.............187

    Chapter Twenty-Four: Baby Name Reveal......................195

    Chapter Twenty-Five: Zigzagging the Parking Lot..........202

    Chapter Twenty-Six: Mailbox Reformation....................212

    Chapter Twenty-Seven: Permanently Temporary or

        Temporarily Permanent 218

    Chapter Twenty-Eight: Finishing Well 225

Epilogue: What to Leave Behind?..234

Acknowledgements..237

About the Author 242

Introduction

What is it about the thought of God's crazy peace surrounding you that can sustain and carry you through anything? And what is it about hearing someone else's true stories of faith and trust that can inspire you to believe God could lavish His loving presence in your life as well?

These are the questions running through my mind as I imagine you reading about the dramatic, funny, and sometimes outrageous events that have taken place in my life. But I also see you thinking, wondering, and pondering about God's hand at work in your life. Would He? Could He? Will He use you for His glory in your everyday events? The answer is a loud and resounding, "Yes!"

Never doubt that the Creator of the Universe gives thought to you, for He is intimately acquainted with all your ways—He cares about the small as well as the big concerns weighing on you. He wants to carry your loads and help you see the hidden opportunities of His touch in your everyday recurrences. Jesus said it best, "Come to

Me, all who are weary and burdened, and I will give you rest. Take My yoke upon you and learn from Me, for I am gentle and humble in heart, and you will find rest for your souls. For My yoke is comfortable, and My burden is light." Matthew 11:28–30.

If you are worried that your faith is too weak or that you've failed to meet some imagined spiritual standard to earn God's love, cast those false illusions aside. At times I've fallen prey to both of these anxieties myself. Some of my outcomes ended humorously, but other situations required a heaping helping of God's mercy and grace. The following examples are living proof that God is absolutely willing to do so much more *with* us and *through* us than we could ever believe is possible. How can we not love Him for that?

One lesson I've learned, my reader friend, is through all of life's ups and downs, God exposes the greater calling He desires for us. He wants us to walk in the Spirit with Him, expecting that we would see Him work in our daily lives, even using vessels such as you and me for His glory. It is possible to learn to act with bold assurance, knowing the reality of an unseen God who lives in and through us, as we look for Him to work in our midst. He always shows up and He loves to show out.

As I consider what my last days on earth might look like, and think about finishing well, I am surrounded by

God's crazy peace. None of us know when our final moment might come, but when we put our faith in the Almighty, we can live every last second with unflinching assurance. Not only will we have an amazing and indescribable future in eternity, but we too, will leave a legacy that reaches far beyond our days on this planet.

I invite you to read the testimonies I've shared in this book with others, so you can explore and engage in conversations together. At the end of each chapter, you will find "Opening Our Eyes" questions formulated for deeper discussions. I yearn for you to see and believe and experience for yourself the power of walking with our all-powerful God. So dig in and experience His crazy peace—then pass it on to whomever you may meet.

Tightly wrapped in His embrace,

Linda

SECTION 1

God's Crazy Peace
of Protection

CHAPTER ONE

Angelic Incognito

*S*urely these things happen to everyone—or do they? Maybe others are just not writing them down. But I am. These thoughts have skirted through my brain many times.

Since those early musings, I've discovered not everyone "sees" the supernatural workings behind our everyday events. I still wonder if we don't need reminders to open our eyes, so we can look for God's daily touches in our lives. For me, I've experienced too many dramatic circumstances to ignore the truth that we are never alone, especially in our most terrifying moments. One particular incident comes to mind.

At seven months pregnant, I headed to the mall on a mission to buy school clothes with my two young sons. I left early in hopes of beating the height of Georgia's August heat, my two- and six-year-old sons buckled in the backseat. I typically drive with a lead foot, but not on this particular day. Though I didn't realize it at the time, God was obviously slowing me down, reducing my pedal pressure and causing me to linger a little longer at a stop sign.

During my hesitation at the intersection, a heavy-duty log truck zoomed past me. I made my turn behind him, traveling down the hilly terrain of Georgia Highway 120. I lost sight of the logger, driving carefully on the two-lane road as it dipped up and down like a seesaw. I smiled at the sounds of giggles coming from the back seat, each time my little sons felt the stomach rush of driving the asphalt peaks and valleys.

I topped yet another hill, only to have the smile immediately fade from my face. I could easily see what was ahead, but my mind struggled to register the reality. My foot instinctively snapped from the gas to the brake. An 18-wheeler crept slowly across the highway, cutting into the opposing lane—my lane. By the time he noticed and began to correct, I knew he wasn't going to make it before our paths intersected. The log truck in front of me was now my only hope, taking up the space between the big rig and me.

The monstrous log truck swerved, but not soon enough to move its bulky frame out of impact zone. When the two massive vehicles struck each other, the sound of screeching tires and scratching metal was deafening. I vigorously pumped my brakes, slowing my car, but helpless to keep myself out of harm's way. Neither could I influence the unfolding slow-motion scene I was witnessing.

In the final, lingering seconds before my unstoppable collision, I watched the log truck cut the 18-wheeler's axle in half, causing both vehicles to careen outside of my perimeter. Much of the rig's loaded boxes scattered like litter along the highway, some landing mere feet from my front bumper. Each part of the 18-wheeler's two halves finally came to rest behind the log truck. Thankfully, the semi's cab with the driver inside was completely intact. The log truck hadn't fared so well.

Overcome with relief that we were spared I steered my car to the shoulder of the road. After double-checking to ensure my sons were safe, concern for the driver of the log truck engulfed me. I quickly opened my car door and assured my boys, "Mommy will be right back. It's all right."

On weak legs, I scurried over to check on the logger, not that I could do much for him. I was thrilled to find him alive, though his attempts to apply the brakes had left him pinned in his cab, frozen in a standing-up position.

"Are you okay?" I said.

The man's eyes were round with terror. "Lady, I can't feel my legs!"

All I could offer him were my encouragements, prayers, and compassion, which was exactly what he needed. Soon, a quietness came over him. The driver and I were talking calmly when the sound of people rushing all around us interrupted. Other passersby had arrived.

I continued to pray silently while some men worked their efforts in an attempt to free the logger. Miraculously, someone had a car phone (this was 1983, long before everyone carried their cell), and called the authorities. In only a short couple of minutes, the first sirens sounded in the distance, soon followed by bright flashing lights in orange, blue, yellow, and red.

EMTs spilled out of an ambulance and rushed to the log truck, while a trooper stepped authoritatively from his cruiser. Those of us first on the scene, who had tried our best to help the logger, were instructed to clear the road immediately. We had to make room for more emergency vehicles. I never saw what happened to the driver of the 18-wheeler, but based on the undamaged condition of his cab, I can only guess he was mildly injured at worst.

I returned to my car, got in, and twisted toward the back seat, facing my children. My six-year-old, who regularly made up his own words, held up his shaky hands. "Mama, my hands are 'crilling.'"

Assuming he meant he couldn't stop trembling, mine were "crilling," as well.

After tending to my boys, I sat silently while emergency services did their thing. My mind swirled. I couldn't stop processing what I had just witnessed. Then another amazing fact struck me.

We had received additional protection. There were no other vehicles traveling toward us on the other side of the busy, two-lane road, which was miraculous. Even after the collision, any vehicle coming south on Highway 120 would have hit the rear end of the 18-wheeler. The impact with some of those large freight boxes strewn all over the highway might have thrown them right onto my car. Just imagining those alternative scenarios made me shudder— thankful that God had been with us.

I couldn't wrap my mind around the protection I had just experienced. I continued to thank God over and over for our safety. He had physically shielded us from tragedy, thereby allowing us to escape unscathed. And yet, the miracles kept coming.

I didn't think about it until a few days later. I never heard what happened to the log truck driver. Were they able to extricate him without causing further damage to his body? How severe were his injuries? Would he be able to walk again? The realization that I'd let him slip from my mind convicted me. I had to make this right. I wanted to let him know that his actions had saved our lives and I was grateful. I also wanted to tell him about Jesus, so I made a few calls.

My stomach fluttered with nerves when I dialed the first number. A man with a matter-of-fact voice answered. "Duluth City Police, may I help you?"

"I witnessed the accident on Highway 120 the other day, between the 18-wheeler and the log truck. I wondered if I could get some information."

"Let me pull up the report." For several minutes, the sound of shuffling papers and file folders echoed in the background. The officer finally spoke. "Um, ma'am, I see one 18-wheeler incident on Highway 120 in the past week, but I have no record of a log truck's involvement in the wreck. Actually, I don't see any recent reports with log trucks. Are you sure the accident happened in our jurisdiction?"

"I'm positive," I said. "I was right there and watched the whole thing. Would it be too early for the report to be filed?"

"No ma'am. Our officers submit their reports as soon as they're complete."

Perplexed, I thanked the officer and ended the call. Maybe it was a county matter, though I was sure the accident had taken place at the edge of the Duluth, Georgia city limits.

I next called the Gwinnett County Sheriff's Department. After looking through their files, they essentially said the same thing, "We have no recent record of an accident involving a log truck, but a semi crashed on your date."

Finally, I contacted the Georgia State Highway Patrol, but to no avail. None of the three law enforcement agencies had a record of a log truck driver in an accident on

Highway 120. It was as if the intervening vehicle did not exist—except I knew it had. The situation left me to ponder.

Was this possibly an angelic sighting?

Could I have met and spoken to my first angel ever?

Could he have been driving a log truck?

I may be stretching things, but I can only assume that my divinely dispatched protector had "log truck driving" on his resume. That close call definitely confirmed the absolute existence of angels to me. And the whole experience made me want to separate truth from myth.

I turned to the Bible, my go-to book for clarifying and rightly dividing fiction from fact. In my studies, I discovered some common misconceptions about celestial beings.

1. Nowhere does the Bible say angels are people who died and became heavenly highflyers. (God made both human beings and angelic beings for His very unique purposes.)

2. Angels are not cute chubby babies with tiny wings. (I wonder which sculptor or artist created that visual? Possibly Michelangelo?)

3. Angels do not *earn* their wings. (The legend of a bell-ringing wing assignment came from the movie, *It's a Wonderful Life*. But did the idea exist before the big screen, or was the notion created for a good storyline?)

In fact, the Bible clearly says angels are sent to earth, serving God as His messengers, guardians, trumpet blowers, warriors, and even worshipers. I'm convinced my angel served in the guardian regiment and was sent to protect my family and me. Otherwise, we would be in heaven today.

Even as I type these incredible details, I feel compelled to whisper another grateful prayer for the miracle of God's provision. On that August afternoon, He allowed me, my unborn baby, and my two sons to drive safely through the path of an 18-wheeler, totally unscathed.

For me, the "not-of-this-earth" event verified the reality of God, who is able to do exceedingly, abundantly beyond all I could ask, think, dream, or hope. Although the experience was mind-baffling, it served as concrete proof that nothing is impossible with Him. My eyes were opened wider than ever that day.

God, in His heavenly realm, has been endlessly watching over all of His children, day and night, 24/7, since the beginning of time. I envision a plethora of angelic beings, standing in mighty wing-to-wing formations. They wait for God to summon them into His presence—their main mission to serve and protect us. It's amazing to me that we never notice even the hint of a stirred breeze as they obediently set out to accomplish His requests, often on our behalf.

Being omniscient, God needn't peer over the side-arm of His throne to view any scene, including the accident that unfolded on Highway 120 in August 1983. He knows all and sees all, in advance. Before the first screech of tires, I believe He issued a protective communique on my behalf, dispatching the most perfectly equipped angel to move all elements of danger from my path.

It's overwhelming to think there's nowhere you or I can wander beyond God's watchful eye. He exists outside of all space and time limitations, and the comforting truth is that His care is unyielding. We cannot control much of anything. But understanding that God orchestrates every outcome of our lives, including the dates of our deaths, can help us breathe and lean into faith.

On any given day, we go about our business mostly unaware of the shielding we receive, especially if we do not ask God to open our eyes to see what He is doing for us. We must remain on the lookout for the supernatural in everyday events, where assigned angels surround us and keep danger at bay. It is in the seeing where one of God's greatest gifts—gratitude—comes to life. In truth, we all have much to be thankful for, but we first must overcome our fears.

Opening Our Eyes

1. Do you truly trust God with your every moment—
   especially the terrifying ones? Do you fear death,
   or are you confident you will spend eternity in
   heaven? Why or why not? *My times are in Your hand*
   (Psalm 31:15a).

2. Have you ever experienced a close call or near
   death? When you reflect back, viewing the situation
   with spiritually open eyes, can you see where God
   may have sent an angel or two on your behalf? . . .
   He will give His angels orders concerning you . . .
   (Matthew 4:6).

CHAPTER TWO

Babysitting Betsy the Ballet Boa

Enmity—defined as a mutual hatred. Enmity precisely describes what God placed between the woman and the snake in the Garden of Eden, so long ago.

For me, hatred perfectly defines my relationship with slithering creatures. There are no "good" snakes, and that's my final thought on the subject. Even my husband, Mac or Mackey as I called him, could not reassure me of their good qualities, though he tried. More than once the subject caused a debate between us. One comes to mind.

I'd spotted the vile offender when its ebony skin glinted under the summer sunlight near the flowers I was tending. I shrieked and ran inside, locking the door behind me. I did not want that reptile coming anywhere near my vicinity.

Mackey, who'd heard my screams, ran into the room. "What happened?" A look of concern furrowed his features.

Still panting, I dared not move my back away from the door. "There's. A snake. In the yard!"

"Where?" Mac said.

"Near the hydrangeas. It's stretched out along the foundation of the house. You've got to kill it," I spat.

"Calm down. What color is it?"

"Calm down? How am I supposed to calm down when there's an uninvited creature in my flowerbed?" I pushed away from the door and stepped closer to my husband, frustration overtaking my fear. "It's black—and really long."

Mackey held his arms out for me to fall into. "Okay, okay," he soothed. "Let me go see what variety it is, and then I'll decide what to do with it."

I removed myself from the comfort of my husband's embrace and put my hands on my hips, squaring off with him. "Are you kidding me? You'll decide what to do with it? I told you what we need to do—kill it!"

Ignoring my directive, Mac moved toward the door. I opened my mouth to protest, but he interrupted. "I'll be right back. Just let me see what we're dealing with." He slipped outside before I could argue more.

A few minutes later, Mac came back inside. "Honey, that's a black kingsnake, and we want it to live in our backyard. It preys on all of the venomous snakes."

"Sorry, Mackey, there's nothing you can do or tell me that will change my position on the subject. I don't care what you call His Royalty, Mr. Kingsnake. It does not impress me in the least, nor does his supposed job description bring me any comfort. He's a serpent, and I loathe him as much as Eve must have hated the serpent who deceived her in the garden."

Eventually, my pleas and pressure worked. Mac begrudgingly removed the snake. I peeked through my curtains, watching my husband gingerly pick up the black beast and carry it off. I did not want to know where.

I tell you this so you will understand the depth of my seriousness when I offer the tale of the most challenging task ever requested of me. The fear was real.

My husband and I loved to watch our daughter, Bethany, perform. She's a professional ballerina who toured the world dancing while sharing Christ's love. Being proud parents, we showed up at most of her venues, although this one dance program presented a problem. It was only two hours south of us, but the event happened to be on the same day my husband was to return from his six-week business project. We felt the scheduling conflict of the two significant events was too much to handle. Therefore, we didn't plan on attending the performance.

Mac, however, also known as the "dance dad of all dance dads," searched until he found an earlier flight. He decided we could make it on time.

I called Bethany to give her the update and ask for location details. She picked up on the second ring. "Hey, Mom," she said.

The sound of her voice made me smile. "I've got good news. Dad is arriving earlier than scheduled, so he and I are planning to come to Natchez to your show at the community center."

"That would be great. We're still on the bus, but almost to the venue."

I heard John, a dancer, in the background. "Can I talk to your mom a sec?"

First hearing some rustling sounds, John's voice came on the line. "Hi Linda, you and Mac are coming to watch *Deliver Us* in Natchez, right? I wondered if I could ask a favor."

"Sure," I said naively.

"Could you please stop by my house, get Betsy, and bring her with you?"

I swallowed, trying to loosen my tongue, which seemed to instantly swell when I heard John's request. I couldn't believe this. I had not yet met Betsy, but I knew who she was. Betsy the Boa Constrictor would add the perfect degree of authenticity to Bethany's show. Why shouldn't the Pharaoh's Palace scene in *Deliver Us* have a slimy serpent slithering around?

John waited quietly during my extended pause. Not only was I trying to make my tongue work, but I needed to request divine intervention. "Why me, God? Can't you choose someone else to help John?" I begged answers from the Almighty.

I had a spiritual sense that no answer was my answer, but it was not what I wanted to hear. Without a legitimate reason to say no, I buckled under the pressure. I made my mouth move and reluctantly said, "Sure, John, I can do that. Tell me what I need to know." I couldn't even believe this was me speaking.

John assured me. "My son, Joseph, will have Betsy securely bound in her box. No need to worry about anything."

I felt a shiver of fear climb up my spine. *Doesn't he know we are talking about a snake?* I finished the call in a daze, as John and I set a time for the serpentine transfer to occur.

I tried to keep my mind busy in an effort to escape the dread I felt every time I imagined picking up the snake (not literally with my hands—that was *not* going to happen). I had no idea how long it would take me to go by John's to get Betsy, then swing by the airport to pick up my honey.

When I arrived at John's house, I foolishly expected to be greeted by Joseph with a padlocked metal box, keeping the snake I feared so much safely out of my sight. But instead, the blonde-haired, freckle-faced boy swung the front door open wide with a giant Boa dangling from his neck. I confess I might have gasped.

"Uh. Hi, Joseph." I stumbled over my words, more timid than usual. I had to conjure up all my strength to fight the urgent compulsion to turn and run as far and fast as possible away from the house.

Frozen in place, I watched in horror as Joseph peeled Betsy off his neck, coiled her up, and secured her in her box—a cardboard box—secured with mere cellophane tape. "Want me to put her in your vehicle for you?" Joseph said.

My voice croaked. "I would appreciate it."

After putting Betsy in the back, Joseph shut the hatch on my van. There was no turning back, the snake was now inside my vehicle. "There ya go," he said. "Just be sure to check every once in a while to see that she doesn't escape under your feet while you're driving." He laughed. I did not.

Teasing or not, Joseph's warning drove my fear intensity to an unhealthy extreme. Although my slithering cargo was supposedly secure, my mind flooded with images of Betsy trying to escape the confines of the box. *God, help me,* I prayed silently.

The reptile exchange had taken place much quicker than I anticipated, which left me with forty-five minutes to kill before heading to the airport. How was I going to fill the gap?

Speaking to myself, but loud enough for Betsy to hear as well, I said, "I love to read. I could pass the time with a book." But I wasn't keen on remaining in the van with such a volatile package for company.

I continued my one-sided conversation. "Betsy, are you happy coiled up in your box?"

I waited, but no comment wafted up from her cardboard containment.

"Have you ever escaped before?" I did not want an answer to that one. What if she really could escape? Questions such as these made me strain for a solution to my timing dilemma. *What can I do while I wait for Mackey's arrival?*

I searched my mind for a legitimate excuse to exit my "snake-infested" van. I decided a coffee shop could provide just the safe escape I needed from this snake-y prison on wheels.

After I parked, I peered in the rear window of my van. Thankfully, the tape still held firm.

Thirty minutes later, I looked through my window again. The box was still secure. Relief replaced that familiar shiver of fear traveling up and down my spine. All was well. Phew!

After a quick stop for gas, where I did a third check to make sure Betsy was secure, I started for the airport. I pulled up to the terminal, parked, and checked the board for my husband's flight. I was never so glad my knight in shining armor was landing on time.

After we got his bags and were walking to the van, it occurred to me I'd forgotten to tell my husband about the snake shuttle. As we got to our vehicle, I knew I needed to rectify the situation. "Mackey, I have something to tell you. Wait before you open the trunk."

He stopped and looked at me strangely, waiting for me to explain. Knowing me as he most certainly did, he could not have predicted what I was about to tell him.

I leaned with my back to the trunk to stop him from opening the hatch-back. "We have a very unwelcomed passenger hidden away back here. I agreed to a strange delivery job for John."

Not waiting for further clarification, Mac gently moved me aside and opened the back of the van. He lifted his oversized suitcase and heavy backpack into our trunk, carefully avoiding the cardboard box with Betsy inside. He didn't seem phased, as he nestled his bags right up next to the reptilian package. I guess the adventure of living with me for so many years left little concern for my latest surprise.

We then headed south for Betsy's cameo performance with not a minute to waste. We had just enough driving time for the curtain rise in two hours. I explained the reason for our passenger on the way.

Although Mac was now with me, I found the ride far from relaxing. During the entire trip, I battled the urge to pick my feet off the floorboard and hug my knees tightly to my chest. I kept picturing Betsy's scaly body slithering under my seat. It made me edgy and not the best travel companion.

When we got to the venue, we drove around to the stage door. Mac quickly grabbed the Betsy box and delivered it to the waiting stagehand, bringing great relief to my soul. We had five minutes to spare before the curtain call. Betsy would have just enough time to "primp and freshen up" (if she did such things) before her palatial scene, where she would lie at the feet of Pharaoh in all his splendor.

While we walked to our seats, I reflected on how imprisoned I'd felt over the past few days. I was especially disappointed that I let fear take the joy from my drive with Mackey. I'd missed him. Just before the program started, I leaned near Mac's ear and whispered. "Honey, I'm so thankful you're home again. And I'm sorry I allowed myself to be shackled in anxiety throughout our whole ride together. Would you forgive me?"

"Sure, Babe." He squeezed my hand.

My husband had no idea what I had put myself through, imagining worst-case scenarios that never took place. Instead of using my eyes to allow God to show me His crazy peace, I allowed my mind to concoct various possibilities. My unfounded fear proved the acronym by the same name, credited to an unknown author. FEAR: False Evidence Appearing Real.

Although God had watched over me while I babysat Betsy the Ballerina Boa, I most assuredly didn't feel like much of an overcomer. I'd temporarily forgotten that God's Word is powerful enough to protect me and my joy. Just because a snake needed to hitch a ride south, I let fear ruffle my feathers. Shame on me.

There's no way to recover a full day of lost joy, except to learn from it. If like me, you find yourself succumbing to anxiety or unwarranted concern, or frankly, a reasonable reason to fear, don't waste any more time and energy beating yourself up. Give yourself some grace and resolve to do better next time. When fear knocks on our hearts, we can remember to look at the situation through spiritual eyes and take our thoughts captive. God always offers crazy peace—we must simply decide to accept it. But first, we must choose to hear.

Opening Our Eyes

1. Can you remember a time when you allowed fear (fake evidence appearing real) to overtake you, resulting in stolen joy? Can you walk through that memory in your mind thinking through at which point could you have asked God for help, resulting in having your joy restored? *The Lord is my light and my salvation; Whom should I fear? The Lord is the defense of my life; Whom should I dread?* (Psalm 27:1).

2. Which Scripture verses have helped you most in times of high anxiety, worry, or fear? When have you successfully taken a thought captive and overcome your difficult emotions? *We are destroying arguments and all arrogance raised against the knowledge of God, and we are taking every thought captive to the obedience of Christ* (2 Corinthians 10:5).

CHAPTER THREE

Can You Hear Me Now?

If you yearn to hear even the faintest whisper of the Almighty, be prepared for His instruction to ... *Be still, and know that I am God* ... (Psa. 46:10, NIV). His voice can come as a mere whisper, so gentle at times, that it can take you by surprise—unless you are intentionally listening for it.

It was 1979, and I had no idea God had signed me up for a private session in the art of "Listening 101." I'd just come out of a weekend full of conversations and much laughter, while my mother, aunt, and sister visited us in our new home. The southern goodbyes had been spoken, the kisses and hugs were expended, and finally, the routine of endless waving completed, as they drove out of sight.

The afternoon sun streamed through the trees, and my husband decided this was the perfect time to take a quick ride on his ten-speed bike. Our two-and-a-half-year-old son, Doug, entertained himself with toys in his bedroom, within earshot. I decided to head to the spare room and finish a sewing project.

My neighbor had taught me to sew Doug's play clothes out of knit material. Remember, this was 1979, the era of polyester, corduroy, and knitted fabrics. As my machine buzzed away, I slipped into a mysterious sewing zone, where I lost my mommy sense for checking in on my precocious son. All seemed so right with the world. I was clueless that I was headed for a serious life-lesson. God would soon teach me that He does speak, I just needed to be still enough to hear Him.

While sewing, I "heard" in my heart of hearts that I was about to receive a phone call from someone I didn't know. That's odd, I thought. But immediately tuned the inner voice out. Things got more bizarre when the phone immediately began to ring.

In the Seventies, there was no need to search through my purse, or run room to room looking for the telephone. It was securely mounted on the kitchen wall, where it always stayed. I pulled the receiver from the base. "Hello," I said. "Who's calling?"

"This is Joanne. You don't know me, but I'm Susie's mom. She babysat for your son, Doug."

"Yes, how are you?" I struggled to stay focused on the caller. I was still rattled by the fact that my phone rang right after I received the message in my spirit alerting me it would happen.

The woman's voice interrupted my thoughts. "I'm actually at home with the flu, but I was sipping tea at my kitchen table when I spotted Doug on his tricycle heading toward Nailor Road."

My mind scrambled, beginning to register what the woman was telling me. Nailor was a medium-to-busy street off the main highway—nine houses away from ours.

She continued, "I tried to get him to come inside, but since he doesn't know me, he refused. I sent him back toward your house."

I gasped. "Thank you, so very much!" Not waiting for a reply, I hung up the phone and flew out the front door, running toward the corner. Because my street was a bit hilly, I didn't spot Doug until he finally pedaled to the highest point. When the top of his head broke the skyline of my view, tears of relief streamed down my face.

Oblivious to my panic, Doug's little legs circled round and round on his red Radio Flyer tricycle. I watched in disbelief, stunned that my toddler had traveled such a far distance. Then I praised God. "Thank you for not letting me lose my one and only son." As soon as the words left my lips, I thought about how God the Father might have felt when His son was tortured and died.

Did God shed tears of agony as Jesus was stripped, flogged, hammered, hung to die, and buried in a darkened grave for three days? I don't doubt that God the Father yearned to snatch His Son back up to the safety of His presence. But our sins demanded death as payment, and Jesus was willing to pay the price for us. On that third day, though, what joy God must have felt when the earth began to shake, and His one and only Son rose to victory! And how did God react when He held His boy in His arms again? Bending down and scooping up my precious freckle-faced towhead, I felt like I had an inkling.

I couldn't decide what to do first. Should I shower Doug with hugs, or begin the stern talk? I went with the latter.

"Doug, what on earth were you thinking? That was dangerous. You're not allowed to ride your bike in the street. How many times have I warned you?"

"I was just trying to follow Dad." Tears streamed down Doug's freckled cheeks.

Something about Doug's declaration made me realize that his disobedience was no worse than mine. God had clearly spoken to me while I was sitting at the sewing machine. But I initially shrugged His voice off and treated it with no more regard than a fleeting thought. I had unintentionally closed my eyes, and it almost cost me everything. I immediately began to pray silently.

Lord, forgive me. In spite of my disregard, You faithfully watched over my son and me. You assigned angels to guard us, and You gave me a warning message, even before I realized that we needed protection.

I learned a great lesson that day, in my private session of "Listening 101." God confirmed that He sees me, guards me, and speaks to me. Most importantly, He patiently communes with me, even when it takes more than once for this sheep to "hear His voice." Crazy peace comes when we are intentional to really listen, for our own protection. Otherwise, we may end up in the wrong place. God is ever asking, "Do you really know where you are?"

Opening Our Eyes

---

1. Have you heard God lately, and if so, what did He say to you? Have you recognized His still, small voice, whispering truth and guidance to you? *Listen and hear my voice, Pay attention and hear my words* (Isaiah 28:23).

2. Do you keep your life so full of busyness that it is difficult to hear God? Do your calendar and commitments ever make you forget that God is in control and waiting to protect you and yours? *Stop striving and know that I am God* (Psalm 46:10a).

CHAPTER FOUR

Chinese Jewelry Heist

What would you do if your doorbell rang, and two ladies pushed their way into your house in broad daylight saying, "We're just here for the jewelry."?

This was the dilemma of an elderly man of Chinese descent. Thankfully, the poor frightened soul didn't pull a gun on us, uh, I mean on them, or keel over with a heart attack. Okay, I admit that I was awkwardly involved in the above scenario.

It all started on a sunny day in June 2015 when my friend, a dance teacher, Tracey, received an invitation. Did her ballet troupe want to perform for a women's special event?

This invite was an honor, as well as an opportunity to stretch Tracey's students' skills and confidence. Tracey knew that since it was summer vacation, she would be challenged to find six dancers who knew the routine and were in town to participate.

She began calling her best and most prepared girls, relieved to quickly find five who had performed the dance in their May recital. Tracey's hunt continued, looking for that one last dancer who knew the choreography. The young woman's affirmative answer sealed the deal and the troupe of six began rehearsing.

Tracey also had to confirm costumes. Five of the dancers had all of their pieces, including the matching jewelry needed to bring the outfit all together. A borrowed costume for the sixth dancer fit perfectly, but the jewelry was missing. The search was on. Tracey contacted a former dance mom, Mrs. Li, whom we both knew.

Mrs. Li happily agreed to loan her daughter's matching jewelry to the dancer. Tracey just had to pick it up. She asked me to ride along.

The scheduled day for getting the jewelry came and Tracey pulled into my driveway right on time. I hopped in anticipating a fun excursion with my friend. I did not comprehend just how adventurous our day would become. The conflict started before we backed out of my drive.

Tracey said, "Could you put the address into my GPS? It's 426 Emerald Drive."

I hesitated. "I think it's 462 Emerald Drive. I dropped something off to Mrs. Li at her house not that long ago."

"I know she told me 426. Look, I wrote it down," Tracey said, picking up a small piece of paper with a handwritten street address on it. She passed it to me.

Sure enough, the number on the paper was 426. But I'd just been there and felt confident it was 462. "Could you have written it down wrong?" I said.

There was a tinge of confusion in Tracey's voice when she spoke. "I'm sure that's what she told me."

Thinking my friend might be right and I might be wrong, I deferred. I punched 426 Emerald Drive into the GPS, and we backed onto the street. I let the matter go and we enjoyed a pleasant drive with lots of laughter and chit-chat.

Fifteen minutes later, the GPS directed us to the same subdivision I'd recently visited. The area looked right, but I still had that uneasy feeling and I sensed I should speak up again. But I questioned myself more than the spiritual gut-check and said nothing.

We pulled up to 426 and got out of the car. I still had my doubts, but Tracey boldly strode the sidewalk and rang the doorbell.

A very frail, elderly Asian man sheepishly cracked open the door. He peered out, just enough to see our faces.

"Hi," Tracey said. "We're just here for the jewelry."

The man stared at us.

Tracey tried again. "Is Mrs. Li home?" she said brightly.

Again, no comment.

Tracey turned her attention to me for a moment and whispered. "He must be Mrs. Li's dad or father-in-law, but I don't think he understands English."

I nodded my agreement. "Let me try," I said, wanting to help.

Speaking loudly to the man, as if he were deaf instead of non-English speaking, I mimicked my words with hand motions. "Mrs. Li is loaning us jewelry." I put my fingers to my earrings touching them, then gestured a necklace placement, patting as if I were smoothing it in place.

The man blinked his eyes at me. Otherwise, he did not even move.

Tracey took over again. This time, she became more adamant and matched the loudness of decibel I had used. "We need to come inside," she waved her arm broadly, pointing to the living room just beyond the man's body. "We'll just let Mrs. Li know we're here." In a cat-like sweep, Tracey circumvented the man, stepping into the house, and motioned for me to follow.

The man silently turned his body to follow my movement as I shadowed Tracey into the living room. I huddled closely to my friend, feeling awkward.

"Mrs. Li," Tracey shouted, "we're here to pick up the jewelry."

I noticed the Asian man's face now looked startled. His eyes were rounded, and I wondered if he was going to cry.

Tracey didn't appear to notice him and looked at me, "Maybe she's in one of the bedrooms." My friend marched down the hall and opened a couple of doors, peering into each room. "Mrs. Li? Are you back here?"

Looking absolutely startled now, the man finally began to speak. But though the emotion behind his elevated words was obvious, we could not understand what he was saying.

Tracey, oblivious to the man's jabbering, continued moving from room to room. After she'd checked each one for Mrs. Li's presence, Tracey rejoined us in the living room. She shrugged at me and opened her mouth to speak, but she didn't get the first word out.

Speaking much more rapidly now and motioning with jabs and thrusts, it was clear the man was stirred up. When he pointed his finger toward the front door, however, adding a sharply repeated message in what we could only assume was Chinese, we understood his meaning loud and clear. The man was telling us to leave the house. Immediately!

"We're not here to upset you," Tracey tried to explain. "We're just here for the jewelry Mrs. Li said we could borrow."

The man pointed more vehemently toward the door, and in a raised voice, repeated what we could only interpret as "Get out!"

Tracey and I dashed for the door, both apologizing profusely, though the man had no clue that's what we were doing. Seconds later, we stood on his sidewalk, confused and disappointed. We were at a dead end, leaving without the needed bling.

"Why don't you call Mrs. Li and see where she is?" I offered.

"I was just thinking the same thing," Tracey said, pulling her phone out of her purse.

Only hearing Tracey's side of the conversation with Mrs. Li, I could still tell what the problem was. But I waited for my friend to get off the phone and give me the details.

When she ended the call, Tracey rolled her eyes at me. "Oh dear. Mrs. Li's street address is 462 Emerald Drive, not 426. Mrs. Li knows this man, and he is of Chinese descent like her, but he's no relation. We just invaded this man's house and terrorized him, for no good reason. Mrs. Li said she would call and explain our mistake. She said she's sure he won't want to have us arrested."

Yikes, that possibility hadn't occurred to me yet.

After we picked up the jewelry from Mrs. Li, at the right house, we drove home. We relived the whole astonishing experience we'd just shared during the entire drive. Tracey and I cry-laughed and laugh-cried, imagining that sweet man trying to explain us to his family. Their faces must have registered complete shock when he described two strange American women pushing their way into the house, and then going through each room.

Thankfully, he didn't speak English. Otherwise when we told him, "We're just here for the jewelry," he might have thought it was a heist.

At home later, I continued to ponder the situation, and realized there was a spiritual lesson in our unbelievable adventure. I thought about some of my reactions, at times when the Holy Spirit tried to clear up my mistaken thinking.

Okay, I'll confess, I'm not always open to correction—to my detriment. In my refusal to hear the Holy Spirit when He's told me I was wrong not to apologize, to forgive, to listen, to look at a situation through someone else's eyes, to love unconditionally, or a myriad of other sins I've committed, I've caused confusion and chaos for myself. I've also frustrated and hurt others.

Many times, I've closed my eyes to the possibility of my mistakenness and moved away from the opportunity to experience God's crazy peace. This is only one example.

Since our "Chinese jewelry heist," I've learned never to proceed without double-checking the address and don't press in based on your confidence alone. Also, some hand gestures just won't work, no matter how much you flail. This is good advice for any circumstance.

The mistake Tracey and I made could have landed us in jail, and we would have deserved the punishment we received. Thankfully, the man whose house we invaded gave us undeserved grace, much like God gives us every day. When I was a parent, I relearned this insight on a continual basis, in small and big ways.

Opening Our Eyes

1. Can you recall a time when you knew God was leading you in a particular direction, perhaps to apologize when you didn't feel wrong, but you went the other way? Do you wish you would have done anything differently with hindsight? "*For My thoughts are not your thoughts, nor are your ways My ways,*" *declares the Lord* (Isaiah 55:8).

2. Have you ever tried to pick up or take something you believed to be yours, only to find out it belonged to someone else? Has there ever been a time when you found yourself in unwanted conflict or confusion over a possession? *You shall not steal,* (Exodus 20:15).

CHAPTER FIVE

Crisis at the Gas Pump

"**H**ow big is big?"

That's what our young children want to know when we use the abstract term "big" to define the size of something. Their incessant probes to find out what we mean, and to get answers immediately, can make parents want to scream. You've heard a child's drill, as they seek to make sense of the details in their own minds. I'd imagine you've either had a conversation like the one following, or you've heard one.

"Mommy, you said I would understand when I was bigger, but how big is that?"

"Probably when you're big in your twenties."

"How big are twenties?"

"Well, you're four now, but you'll be bigger in twenty years."

"How long is twenty? Will I be bigger like tomorrow?"

"Not tomorrow. In a few years you'll be big."

"But I want to be big tomorrow."

And there lies the crux of the matter—impatience. Wanting immediate results is an issue most of us grapple with starting in childhood. And for some of us, we fight impatience our whole lives.

Think of the little girl who can't wait to be a grownup. She looks so cute, clopping around in Mommy's shoes, playing mother hen to her own pretend children or corporate mama, heading out the door to work. What about the little boy who sticks by Daddy's side as they work on weekend projects? He grips the hammer with two pudgy hands, pushing his father's guidance away, insisting he's big enough to do it by himself. Even if the jobs switch, and the boy pretends to parent or go to work, and the girl helps hammer nails, the inner drive remains the same. Kids are impatient to grow up.

Wise parents train their children to be responsible, and teach them how to do small, even insignificant, chores around the house well before the desire to help dissipates. Sometimes, however, if a parent gives in to a child's impatience, disaster can strike. I learned this the hard way.

We had recently moved from Georgia to Mississippi and spent eleven days living in a hotel with our two-year-old while house-hunting. My first priority was to find the right pediatrician, because our son, Doug, already had an ear infection. This was 1979, so I thumbed through the Yellow Pages and made an appointment with a pediatrician in an ad I liked. I loaded Doug up in the car and we headed out, but soon realized I needed gasoline.

I pulled up to the pump. Doug started in immediately.

"I want to help, Mommy. Let me do it."

"Not this time, honey."

Doug added a distinctive whine to his words. "But I want to."

"No, baby," I stood my ground—if only temporarily.

"But I want to help," Doug shrieked from his car seat. "Let me heeeellllllllp!" His wailing escalated and reverberated not just inside the car, but throughout the entire parking lot.

I relented to Doug's impatient demands quickly, wanting to recover from the embarrassment.

I unhooked my son's car seat belt and carefully placed him on the ground, positioning Doug up against me. I allowed him to place his little hands at the back of the pump handle, while I maintained the main grip. Back then it was not illegal for anyone under sixteen to dispense fuel. I now understand why that law exists.

While the gas pumped, I glanced at the car pulling in across from us. But my attention was forced back in a hurry when Doug started screaming from the depth of his lungs. The scene below me was horrific.

Gasoline had backed up from my full tank and now spewed all over Doug's head. I desperately started swiping my child's eyes in an attempt to protect them, but I was too late to catch it all. Some had dripped in, and Doug's shrills heightened. He began to bat at his eyes yelling, "Owie, owie, Mommy, it hurts!"

I quickly scooped my son up and ran as fast as I could, heading for the door of the convenience store. Some kind soul held it open as I ran inside carrying my screaming, wriggling preschooler.

The clerk led me to the manager's office. I barked out the name of the new pediatrician, and her fingers sped through the pages of the phone book, as she flipped past names, looking for the right doctor. Once she located the pediatrician we hadn't yet met, the clerk dialed the number on the rotary phone, then handed the receiver to me. She took Doug from my arms and ran to the sink to douse his face under a stream of water. I could barely hear the nurse on the phone over my son's screams.

The nurse rushed to tell me, "I need to check with the doctor to make sure we give you the right instructions. I'll be right back."

"Please hurry," I pleaded. But the other end of the phone was already silent.

Those long seconds felt like forever while I waited with Doug crying in agony in the background. "It's okay, baby, Mommy will be right there," I said. I tried to control my rising anxiety, worried that I'd blinded my child for life. I just wanted to hold and comfort him myself.

The nurse finally came back to the phone. "The doctor said to rinse his eyes under running water for at least twenty minutes, getting him to blink frequently in the process."

I repeated (yelled) each part of her instructions to the clerk, who was gently restraining my son in order to keep his eyes under the water. "I think we've been doing that for at least five minutes," I told the nurse.

"Good, that's exactly what he needs. After the twenty minutes are up, come straight in," she said.

I stood up to go to my son when my eyes fell on a small plaque sitting on the manager's desk. It read: *The battle is the Lord's.* Suddenly, it occurred to me that in my nerves, panic, and numbness, I'd forgotten to pray.

This was one battle I was glad to hand over to God. It was much too strenuous for me to fight alone. Not caring who heard me, I prayed out loud as I accepted Doug from the clerk and took over the washing of his eyes. "Lord, You know I'm battling fear and anxiety right now over Doug's eyes. I thank You for beating those feelings back and helping me rest in the assurance of your provision. I praise You for touching my son's body with Your healing hand. In Jesus' Name."

As it turned out, the gasoline did not cause permanent damage. The Lord had gone to battle for both of us. He protected Doug's eyesight and beat back my fear and anxiety with His crazy peace provided through a scripture plaque. However, that was the last time my son helped me pump gasoline, "big" or not.

So how big is "big?" Throughout his younger years, that was the question Doug asked us, over and over when we told him he could not do something until he was bigger. Even as adults, there are situations bigger than us, and like children, we often impatiently wail at God. We demand, scream, and beg, hoping to get our way—looking for the easy answers to our problems or desires. We often operate no more maturely than our kids.

For those of us who've raised children, we understand the need to prayerfully and faithfully persevere in the guarding and training of our little ones. We see the larger picture, beyond their immediate wants, and we understand the details that need to be covered for their safety. God sees things no differently for us.

We are God's children. As we grow, we need to trust Him all the more, creating a healthy cycle of dependence

47

on our Heavenly Father. It's important to realize that He's aware of dangers we don't even know exist, because He is our perfect parent. God wants to give us the desires of our hearts, but only under His protective care.

I can promise you one thing, there will be many crises ahead in life. None of us are immune to conflict, blindsiding events, and moments of panic. However, when we trust Jesus, He becomes our Savior, which means He really will "save us." Even in the case of death, we possess something others are missing—confident hope. Using our spiritual eyes, we realize this world is not our ultimate home, and are given crazy peace as we look ahead to eternity. God's powerful hand is ever at work on our behalf. There's nothing bigger than that, not even when all we can see is blood.

Opening Our Eyes

1. When do you catch yourself leaning on your own understanding, such as experience or education, instead of trusting God? Do you acknowledge that He is the sole source of all wisdom and truth? *Trust in the Lord with all your heart. And do not lean on your own understanding. In all your ways acknowledge Him, And He will make your paths straight* (Proverbs 3:5–6).

2. What circumstances have you faced, bigger than your ability to fix? Do you trust God with everything, or are there any areas you withhold and attempt to handle on your own? *. . . for the battle is the Lord's, . . .* (1 Samuel 17:47).

CHAPTER SIX

Lawn Dart Drama

66 **W**atching my children play together without fighting."
From the women I've known, this would be the
most common poll answer to the question, "What is your
greatest joy as a mom?" Sibling rivalry is a real thing.

When dreaming about becoming a mother, most imagine their little sweethearts caring, sharing, and well, just about anything but bickering. I know I did.

Admittedly, my boys who are four years apart, have engaged in some legendary disagreements ranging from who goes first, to that's my toy, or I had the ball first, etc. Their battles brought me to the edge of exhausted tears many times. But one particular afternoon tops the rest, and it had nothing to do with conflict.

My two precious sons were cooperating and playing together in rare harmony, enjoying a game of lawn darts. They took turns tossing, trying to land inside the ring, good-naturedly ribbing each other in hopes of making the other miss on his turn. If they both landed inside the circle, it canceled both points out.

I pulled the curtain back from my kitchen window and peeked outside at one point, breathing in the scene. I loved seeing my sons play so sweetly, with broad smiles adding a glow to both of their faces. Then I moved my attention back to the macaroni and cheese I was preparing, to go along with my husband's favorite, meatloaf. Minutes later, I pulled the pasta off the burner and replaced it with a small pan of green beans to heat.

The oven timer dinged so I turned it off. Then I carried the meatloaf, mac and cheese, and salad to the table, where my little ones had sort of set it before going to play. I filled the water glasses and looked at the spread with a satisfied smile. As soon as the green beans were done, all I'd need were some hungry males.

I stepped out on the front porch and called for the boys to come inside and wash up. It was beginning to grow dark so the game needed to wrap up soon anyway.

They called back in unison, "Be there in a minute, Mom."

"Hurry up. Supper will get cold," I scolded before returning to the kitchen to toss the salad and grab the green beans. I knew I wouldn't have to nag as darkness would soon chase my sons inside without a second call from me. I had no idea my peaceful evening was about to implode.

A few minutes passed, and my four-year-old, Scott, ran into the kitchen crying. Thinking my sons had finally disrupted their own peace by fighting over something, I barely glanced his way.

"Mommy."

The distress in Scott's voice caused me to turn around. He sounded more upset than just from a brotherly disagreement. The sight of blood pouring from my little boy's mouth caused me to drop the tongs I held in my hands.

Maybe he just lost a tooth, I thought hopefully. After further inspection, I saw he *had* lost a tooth, but he also had a hole in his face, just below his bottom lip.

Desperate and in a bit of shock, I needed assistance. Quick. I started shouting for help, and I was willing to take it from whomever came first.

"Jesus! Mackey! Jesus! Mackey!" I intermittently shouted for my Savior and my husband.

I don't remember turning off the burner, nor do I recall grabbing my two-year-old daughter, but I must have done both. I distinctly remember, however, cuddling Scott while pressing a cloth tightly on his lip to stop the bleeding.

A short time later, we were in the emergency room of our small-town community hospital. The staff showed us as much compassion and kindness as if they'd never seen us before, although visiting the ER was a much-too-common practice with this boy. He was released after stitches were sewn into his face. Finally, we headed home to eat our cold supper.

Two days later, I had to take Scott to the pediatric orthodontist for braces. Though my son was only four, the dentist explained that braces were necessary. He needed to protect Scott's face and gumline, until his permanent teeth emerged.

At the time of our lawn dart drama in 1985, the game was not accompanied by the warning we see on today's packaging. *Not for children* is a message that may have saved countless lives, alerting parents that lawn darts are not a toy.

The medical staff of the local ER already knew Scott on a first-name basis. Even when my eldest son, Doug, broke his arm, the hospital nurses asked, "How's Scott?" before we left. I confess, some of Scott's accidents have made me feel as if I was the target of a lawn dart or two—or on the receiving end of a few biblical direct hits.

God warns us about fiery darts in the Bible's book of Ephesians. When our nemesis, a.k.a. Satan or the evil one attacks, his ultimate mission is always the same. He hopes to sidetrack us with his weapons and draw spiritual blood. His fiery darts may be invisible to us physically, but they are dangerous all the same. If we remain unaware, the enemy of our souls can lead us to a downfall, hurting us and the people we care about.

Isn't it good news to know that God has given us a solution for warding off fiery darts? Opening our eyes means lifting the shield of faith. Our trust in God represents a shield of protection, giving believers power and leading us to a place of crazy peace. The ability to avoid and overcome deadly darts, and thereby live our lives to the fullest, is as easy as allowing God to safeguard us daily. And even if we receive the occasional flesh wound from a dart that got too close, it can serve as a positive warning.

Scott may have a physical scar, but the memory of how he got it offers a great reminder to avoid darts in the dark. When we let down our spiritual guard and choose to live for ourselves versus for God, the enemy recognizes an opportunity. He prepares an onslaught of fiery darts, primed for shooting at our souls. Whether we allow the darkness of doubt or some other temptation to creep in, we may suffer a long-term scar from that single decision.

But when we hold our faith shield high, God promises that we are able to extinguish those spiritual darts—no matter the circumstances. Our secret weapon is trust.

I don't recall whether we ate any of that meatloaf dinner the night of Scott's lawn dart accident, or if we went to bed hungry. But I do know I fell asleep singing songs of praise to God with a grateful heart. That "toy" dart could have left Scott with far worse ramifications than a small scar. God's rescues never end halfway.

Opening Our Eyes

1. When has God been your strength in a situation?
    Do you ever use songs to thank Him for all He has
    done for you? *The Lord is my strength and my shield;
    My heart trusts in Him, and I am helped; Therefore my
    heart triumphs, And with my song I shall thank Him*
    (Psalm 28:7).

2. Have you ever felt as if you were being pummeled
    by fiery darts? When have you successfully held up
    the shield of faith and experienced God's obvious
    protection? *In addition to all, taking up the shield of
    faith with which you will be able to extinguish all the
    flaming arrows of the evil one* (Ephesians 6:16).

CHAPTER SEVEN

Half Is Never Enough

W hen your heartthrob plays football, you automatically become a football player groupie. In my youth, there was this one guy in particular who caught my eye. His family called him Mackey, but sometimes, I called him my "Smack-a-Jack."

Mackey wore the number 53 football jersey. He was the center for the team, and he occupied the center of my heart as well. We met in our sophomore year of high school in 1967.

Wanting to be around him every second possible, I attended all of the games in town and even a few out-of-town ones. I so looked forward to weekends during football season. I admit that before I met number 53, I had no interest in football and knew nothing about the sport, but I soon learned the ins and outs of the game.

Late one night, following our high school football game in the all-encompassing darkness of the New Orleans

City Park, I stood under a grove of mighty oak trees. Their huge sprawling branches created an overhanging canopy that was almost solid, adding to the darkness of the night.

The once-filled stadium of fans and spectators had already headed home, long before the team even made their way from the locker room to the bus. The park looked and felt pretty desolate. But regardless, my practice was to never leave the stadium until I got just one more glimpse of the most handsome center ever. His wave to me, or even the acknowledgement of me by the nod of his head or his eye glancing my way, set my teenaged heart a-flutter. I've wondered if the other jocks ribbed him about my obsession, but if so, he never mentioned it to me.

That night, two of my girlfriends had accompanied me to the game, so at least I wasn't alone. As usual, after the team bus drove out of sight, all that was left was thick darkness.

The branches of the massive oak trees cast shadows around us, creaking in every gust of wind. We felt like we were surrounded by unknown creatures. I don't remember if the moon glowed that night, but even if it had, no moonbeams could penetrate the canopy above us.

When I'd arrived, I had to park my daddy's car pretty far from the stadium gates, and my friends and I dug up enough courage to make the long trek ahead of us. I don't recall our conversation while we walked, but I'm sure I was still pretty giddy from seeing my "Smack-a-Jack." Oh, how puppy love carries you on its wave of innocence.

Finally, we spotted Dad's car, alone in the park. I hunted through my purse for the key and the three of us climbed inside—safe at last! When my fingers grasped its somewhat flimsy, aluminum shape, I pulled it out and placed it into the ignition. I cranked to the right, but immediately heard a snap. Even over our girly chit-chat, my dilemma in the dark became immediately evident to all.

Silence replaced our fun. I sat in disbelief, holding one half of a key while the other half remained stuck in the ignition. How was this even possible?

Fear began to drip all over me. Uninvited questions passed through my brain. *Why did we stay until the very end? Why am I holding one half of a key? How long will it take for us to walk to the concession stand?* I knew we now had to leave the safety of Dad's car and start our solemn walk toward unknown territory and an unwanted adventure.

The depth of darkness felt even blacker as we headed toward the far end of the park. Since it was 1967, we were on a hunt for a telephone booth—housing a large black box with numbers on it. Back then you inserted coins and twirled your fingers round and round the rotary dial, hoping the person you called was near their own phone to answer.

Because of the lateness, there weren't very many head-lights cutting through the inkiness of the park at that hour.

But since desperation had set in, we decided to take a huge risk. My friends and I stuck our three thumbs out and hoped for the best. This is not a good idea today, but it was a different era for children in the Sixties. And today, one wouldn't be hunting for a phone booth either, would one?

I wish I had a memory of the kind soul who picked us up. But we did eventually catch a ride, and safely I might add, to the nearest phone booth. (Whomever you are, thank you for your kindness.)

I stepped inside the booth and pulled the folding doors closed. It scraped the concrete ledge in the process. Then I slid the appropriate amount of coins into the slot and listened as they made their way to my connection. I gulped, because I hadn't really prepared what I'd say to Daddy. But I had no choice, I had to make the dreaded call. His voice startled me out of my meandering thoughts.

"Uh, Daddy?"

"Yes?" At that hour, his yes was accompanied by a hesitant pause, expectant, because whenever I called, he knew I must need help. He called it "another Linda dilemma."

"Dad, can you come and save me? Please? It's not my fault. The car key broke off in the ignition," I said sheepishly. I always hated asking for my daddy's help, although I frequently needed it, and he always gave it. But he did so in his very silent way.

"How's that even possible? Keys don't just break like that. You're telling me you broke the key inside the ignition?" The flatness in my father's voice spotlighted his skepticism.

"Uh, Daddy, I'm holding half a key. And half a key won't work."

"Well, where are you?" He knew my issues meant he wouldn't see the end of whatever TV show he was watching—DVRs didn't exist yet. The "Linda dilemma" interrupted his regularly scheduled program—again.

"I'm in City Park," I said. "At the pay phone."

"I'll be there soon." The click signaled the end of our conversation. But I knew it would take at least twenty minutes for him to arrive. The wait felt like the longest twenty minutes ever.

My guess is that once Dad hung up, he called out to my brother. "Hey Donald, do you wanna go with me to help Linda again?"

My brother, also a consistent savior, would likely have said he would.

I don't remember exactly how Daddy and Donald resolved the situation, but they always helped me out of my ridiculous situations. I'd say they simply brought a spare key, along with a pair of needle-nosed pliers to pull the offending half key out of the ignition. But no matter how they did it, they helped me make it safely home—just like God does today.

The consistent state of crazy peace I live in comes from a mix of faith and history. I trust God to save me, because I have many experiences in my memory bank of Him doing so. I can exercise faith in what He will do for me in my future, because I see so much evidence of His miraculous hand at work in my past. Like my daddy and Donald, I can count on Him to show up. Thankfully though, there's never a need for coins and we don't have to dial.

God watches over us constantly and is always available to come to our rescue. But it's up to us to make that hard call and ask. We might dread telling Him our dilemmas, but in reality, we are never interrupting any regularly scheduled program. We are His highest priority and most important focus.

After my post-football game fiasco, I learned to be gentle with an aluminum key. I'm also especially grateful for push-button ignitions, keyless starters, and cell phones with flashlights. I stand confidently in the knowledge that God is for us and with us, even when what I think I know ends up being something completely different.

Opening Our Eyes

1. Are you confident or fearful about calling on God to say, "Daddy will you save me? Please? Again?" Why do you think people are afraid of calling on God when they are in trouble? *Call upon Me in the day of trouble; I will rescue you, and you will honor Me* (Psalm 50:15).

2. What does it mean to you to be someone who endures to the end? Where could you use God's help today? *But the one who endures to the end is the one who will be saved* (Matthew 24:13).

CHAPTER EIGHT

Olive Jar Bandit

You know the feeling.

It's late and everyone has been fast asleep for hours when all of a sudden, there's a noise! Did something just go "bump in the night?" You freeze, yet your heart races too loudly, as you strain to listen ever so closely. Your imagination soars wildly as your brain attempts to figure out what that sound could possibly have come from.

I remember one particular night where something like this happened to me. I rested peacefully until a loud crash in the kitchen instantly woke me from my sleep. My thumping heart wasn't helped when I leaned over and looked at the time—it was a little after 3:00 in the morning. My mind raced with imaginings. *What could have caused that racket? It must be a burglar.*

I reached for the flashlight I kept in my nightstand drawer, before my feet ever so quietly hit the floor. Without Mac in the house, I had no choice, I had to pretend bravery.

First, I had to be courageous enough to look around the edge of the doorway. I peeked past the frame with only my right eye and half of my head showing, praying the probable burglar could not see me.

Then, against my better judgment, I tiptoed out of my bedroom. I had to see the culprit for myself, no matter how terrified I was. Besides, I had a houseguest, and felt obliged to protect her from harm. Of course, how I was going to do anything more than scream had yet to be figured out.

Again, with only one eye and half a head visible, I dared a glimpse down the hallway. All clear. Now, I just had to make it to the living room and kitchen. One of them was the likely location of my early-morning thief.

I inched my way cautiously through the living room first. All appeared in order, according to my flashlighted view. Then I peered into the kitchen, fully expecting to see the robber in action. I had no idea what I would do after I caught him—I'd figure that out when necessary. I stood silently, awaiting another movement or sound to reveal the robber's precise whereabouts. Ready to pounce, I scanned the room, but saw or heard nothing.

Meanwhile, I spotted my houseguest, Andrea, whose bedroom was on the other side of the kitchen wall. She timidly scrutinized my kitchen from her side of the hallway, with the one eye and half a head protruding position.

I swallowed hard and got up enough courage to whisper, "Andy? I don't see anyone, do you?"

"No," she whispered back. "I don't think there's anyone here."

"Maybe they left," I said.

"I think you're right," she said. "I think it's safe."

I stood up straighter, stiffening my spinal column. "If anyone's in here, you'd better get out. I've got a weapon and I know how to use it," I shouted at the empty kitchen. Only God and I knew my only weapon was the flashlight in my hand. And I wasn't sure I had enough strength to really matter if I cracked someone on the skull with it. I could only hope the false confidence I projected and the sight of me with a wild bedhead and the meanest look I could muster would be enough to cause them to run.

When pure silence met my threats, I took a step into the kitchen, holding my breath until my whole body was fully inside. After I surveyed every corner in the room, I said, "Andy, it's just us." I'd spotted the guilty culprit, and it didn't have two legs after all.

My friend came out of hiding and joined me in the kitchen. What a mess we faced in front of us. It was not the robber we had both conjured up in our mind's eyes, but instead, the origin of the crashing sound came from an inanimate object made of glass.

It was merely an olive jar of all things. But this decorative piece had quite a commanding presence. It stood at eighteen inches high and filled to the corked brim with olives and oil.

I had purchased the distinctive olive jar after I spied it in an indoor flea market and thought it the perfect décor item. I brought it home and was pleased with its stately stance in the corner of my kitchen counter. To give it even more height, I sat it atop a small, plastic bowl turned upside down.

But that very night, "the olive jar bandit" decided enough was enough. I imagined it saying, "I'm not standing on this bowl any longer," then sliding ever so slightly at first, until it slipped off its pedestal. Then it bumped into a ceramic bowl filled with tomatoes and avocadoes, knocking both bowl and jar down, down, down. They landed together with the crashing sound we'd heard, banging onto the tiled kitchen floor below.

At first, my heart sank when I realized my favorite bowl had broken, the one with a Scripture verse along the edge. But on a happy note, the enormous, eighteen-inch jar full of olives and oil somehow remained completely intact. Major mess avoided—thank you, Lord.

So Andy and I began the arduous task of ceramic cleanup at 3:45 a.m. We swept up the tiny shards of splintered glass, but could not do it without uncontrollable giggling, accompanied by short periods of crying. All of our pent-up emotions demanded release. If someone had seen us, they might have wondered if we'd both lost our sanity at the same time.

But even more ridiculous than the laughing and crying, was our attempts at sharing our respective imagined scenarios, causing the mysterious crash. I started.

"When I woke up, I just knew it was a burglar come to clean out my house," I said. "I planned to clunk him over the head with my flashlight. For some reason, it never occurred to me to dial 911."

"Well, my mind didn't go to burglary until you asked me if I'd seen anyone," Andy said. "At first, I thought your dog had escaped his crate and was tearing up the house. I was trying to decide if he would pounce on me, too, or if I was okay to start picking up. Then I saw the top of your head and your eye come around the kitchen corner. It stopped me in my tracks."

I began laughing and said, "At first, all I could see was your eye and part of your face too. You looked like one of those goofy detectives from a private eye comedy."

Each of our belly laughs increased in intensity, and came close to hysteria when we recognized both the commonalities and differing perspectives we each had about the exact same circumstance. Venting our pent-up emotions, the ones that had scared us, and those that gave us joy, provided each of us with a measure of crazy peace.

After we emptied the dustpan, and recovered all of the runaway tomatoes and avocadoes, we returned to our respective bedrooms. It took quite a while before I was able to calm down enough to return to a restful slumber, but after talking things through with God, I finally fell asleep.

Not all sounds that go bump in the night or cause a crash come from scary uninvited guests, or even an escaping dog. Sometimes, an event as mundane as a rebellious olive jar can disrupt our lives. But whatever the source stirring deep emotions, God cares and encourages us to express them.

The Bible tells us to weep when people are weeping. Andy and I did that on my kitchen floor. We are also to laugh with those who are laughing—we did that as well. Who knew that an early morning scenario would help us practice the truth of Ecclesiastes 3:1–8, especially at 3:45 a.m.? At the end of this particular passage, it ends by speaking of peace, a fitting place to rest after emotional lows and highs. When we deal with our feelings now, it prepares us to face whatever is coming next.

Opening Our Eyes

1. Do you allow moments of laughter or do you withhold humor? Has life kicked you in the gut so much that you've lost your ability to see humor in any situation? *A time to weep and a time to laugh; a time to mourn and a time to dance . . . a time to search and a time to give up as lost; a time to keep and a time to throw away* (Ecclesiastes 3:4,6).

2. Have you ever considered God's desire for you to laugh? When was the last time you belly laughed out loud? *He will yet fill your mouth with laughter, And your lips with joyful shouting* (Job 8:21).

CHAPTER NINE

What's Next, Lord? I'm Ready

66 **I**'m ready, Lord. What's next?"

Although those words are simple, easy enough to understand, they were nowhere near my mindset in my teens. That simple statement was years away from ever pouring out of my heart or mouth. I knew moments of crazy peace in my younger years but had not yet experienced the sustained faith that enables me to put absolute, utter, complete trust in God as I face the unknown.

It wasn't until I turned twenty-seven that I became a new creature. I asked God to forgive me and accepted His son, Jesus Christ, as my Savior, and then my transition from worrier to warrior began. Once He got my attention and transformed me, I began to learn about the depth of God's great love for me. He loved ME!

Reality is, God's scale of love is severely imbalanced, leaning heavily in our behalf. When I realized He used that skewed scale to measure and then switch my filthiness to purity through Jesus' sacrifice, making me right with Him, it woke me up to how much I am loved. Think about it, no matter what we've thought, spoken, or done, His Son's blood on that Calvary tree paid the price for our wrongdoing. Christ gave His very life for you and me. And no one looks at us with greater love than God. He sees us at our darkest moments, knowing the healing and blessings He has in store for us if we will only say yes to His plans.

God knew I would need a loving, selfless companion as a husband. So He set into motion the meeting of two teenagers at a high school basketball game in 1967. This laid the foundation for almost fifty years of my crazy peace as Mackey's wife. But I'm getting ahead of myself.

It didn't take long after meeting Mac at the basketball game for he and I to become exclusive. I knew early on that boyfriend of mine was a keeper. He was a diligent student who eventually persevered to become a nuclear field engineer, not an easy task under the best conditions.

After dating through high school and college, we married, and we began what I envisioned as the perfect life. Back then that girl kept her rose-colored glasses tightly in place and could not have imagined some of the bumps and adversities that lay ahead. Does life ever turn out exactly like we plan?

One thing I've always appreciated is Mackey's provision for our family. One of the ways he showed his love for us was through hard work, particularly the sacrifice of traveling for his job. But his dedication paid off in a very successful career. Mac transitioned through various levels of promotions that started early for him. But those doors of opportunity were scattered across many states and included twenty relocations. For a girl who had never been north of Shreveport, Louisiana, Mac's job was a life-changer. Those moves afforded me new possibilities. I met people and visited places I never would have seen otherwise and attended events which greatly enriched my life.

During those moving and re-moving years, we were blessed by the births of our four children. Becoming a mother smoothed over some of the raw edges of my life, as I learned what real sacrificial love felt like. There's nothing like staying up all night with a sick child to show you just what you're willing to give up for someone else. With God's help, my children molded me into the woman only He knew I could become. Though I loved those years, my rose-colored glasses were forced off me more than once. And yet, I learned if you open your eyes to see them, there are tremendous blessings even in the midst of great pain.

Losing my daddy was the first blow to my somewhat perfect life. His passing made me face the reality of death and my own mortality. But even in the depth of my grief, God demonstrated His goodness to me. My dad's death was the catalyst that made me look to God for help the first time. In my weakness, God gave me His strength to lean into, and taught me I could count on Him, no matter what loss I experienced. I missed my daddy terribly but feeling the presence of my Heavenly Father softened my sorrow.

I needed God's comfort a few years later when I grieved a second death, one of unimaginable pain for any young mother. I lost a child in utero. This excruciating event wiped away all that Mac and I looked forward to as we prepared our hearts to welcome one more to love. But suddenly our anticipation turned to agony. The loss of my child stretched my faith, but as I cried and questioned, I also listened for God's response as I read the Bible. A crazy peace began to envelope me. I realized my child had gone ahead of me to those heavenly gates, and someday, those gates would open for me.

When we enter into a relationship with Jesus, our other relationships are affected in the best way. Death has no permanent grip on us. We can look forward to eternal reunions with our lost children and loved ones who also know Christ, when we cross from this life to the next. This confident hope would help me survive my toughest loss yet—though I was spared for thirty more years.

Mackey and I shared the valleys and mountain peaks of living together for almost fifty years. Then suddenly everything I knew about life as a part of a couple was ripped out from underneath me.

Mackey's accidental death stunned me. It also shook my faith like nothing else ever had. I didn't want to enter a totally new avenue of existing without my husband. I didn't want to have to lean on God just to help me crawl out of bed and stumble to the kitchen, forced to face another day alone. I didn't want to feel anger when I saw other couples laugh together or share that intimate knowing glance that speaks a message only they understand. I didn't want the dark nights to come, where a pillow could not replace the warmth of my husband's body next to mine. I didn't want to see with my eyes, that even in this, the worst suffering I'd ever known, God was bringing good from the pain of my intense loss.

During this time, it seems impossible that I never wavered in saying, "You are a good, good God. I trust you to work even this out, according to your higher purpose and plan." But I walked with determination through the necessary stages of grief, and God faithfully stayed with me, during the hard days and bleak nights. I can look back and see how He created beauty out of those ashes. He kept my faith intact. In fact, there has not been a single loss I've endured, where God hasn't shown up and provided for me, often through the hands, feet, and hearts of others.

No doubt, my faith has been tested. But I've learned to live and depend on my God alone. He has faithfully proven to me that He truly is the only one who will never leave or forsake me. He goes before me and behind me, and surrounds me, as surely as the breath I just took. I've grown to know that when adversity hits, God has a greater plan to flesh out with me.

Admittedly, if I had my way, I would bring my husband back. I always pictured growing old with my honey by my side. We hadn't even begun to plan for our retired life together. I always thought we would share in the rewards Mac faithfully saved for, the fruit from his years of labor. But I am not God, and my plans are not so.

Instead, I am learning the truth of Scriptures regarding God's care for the orphan and the widow. These were benefits I never dreamed I'd depend upon, but depend I do. As I face life without my Mackey, I am instead experiencing the provisional love and protection of my faithful God. I have been overwhelmed by the reality of His practical and spiritual care.

God called into service many faithful believers, and some strangers to aid me in my times of need. There is nothing like being on the receiving end when the body of Christ steps up to bring meals, pick up items at the grocery, sit with you when you cry, give you gifts that symbolize God's comfort, listen to you tell the thousandth story about your spouse, and even to fix a broken car or install your new washing machine. I can't tell you how many times I have sat in a puddle feeling all alone, only to have the phone ring or someone show up at my door to offer an encouraging word. Proof of God's existence and unending love is all around me, all I need to do is reflect on the many ways He has sent someone to show me care when I felt helpless and all alone.

Through the pain of losing my husband, I've learned firsthand to open my eyes and look for holy opportunities to be a conduit of God's encouragement, provision, and love. They surround me. Who might I serve? Who needs practical help? Who needs a compassionate and listening ear? Who needs to know they are not alone? Who is grieving? Who needs a helping hand? I find myself continually awestruck that God would include me in His plans as He provides for others, who like myself, were blindsided by an unforeseen kick in the gut. In doing so, I am able to see God transform the pain of my loss to assist in a greater good. It doesn't mean I don't want my husband back or that tears never fall, but this purposeful living gives me crazy peace while I await the day of our heavenly reunion.

Seeing my pain transformed into an eternal benefit is a gift I do not take lightly. For through it, I am able to witness the truth of Romans 8:28. As I watch God provide for each hurting woman I encounter, I witness the bounty of my blessings, overflowing and spilling out, into my small sphere of influence. The trustworthiness of God to carry me faithfully through to my end, which will result in my eternal heavenly home with Him, makes every difficulty bearable.

Battling cancer I again face an unknown future for my time here on earth, however, I do not fear. I know I am held confidently in the hands of a mighty God who knows all. He is the fullness of all wisdom and truth, allowing my heart and soul to settle into that peaceful resting spot, under the wings of my Father.

"What's next, Lord?" I have no idea. But whatever happens, I can boldly say, "I'm ready." God will take care of all my needs, down to what I wear.

Opening Our Eyes

1. Have you ever experienced great pain, and felt like you would never feel better, only to discover a greater purpose because of it? When you reflect back to your times of greatest sadness or grief, can you see where God sent someone to comfort, encourage, or provide for you? *And we know that God causes all things to work together for good to those who love God, to those who are called according to His purpose* (Romans 8:28).

2. How has God allowed you to bless a hurting person(s)? When you help someone in need, how does it make you feel? *Do not merely look out for your own personal interests, but also for the interests of others* (Philippians 2:4).

God's Crazy Peace
of Provision

CHAPTER TEN

Chicken Pox
and a Mini Print Dress

How could a childhood disease affect a fashion statement of the 1980s? It does sound rather bizarre, but I can attest to the possibility as a first-person witness to such an event.

The year was 1983. My friend, Peggy, invited me to a luncheon at a local country club, and it included a free nursery for children. With two little ones underfoot, and few opportunities to enjoy adult interaction, I jumped on the invitation without any hesitation. I clarified with Peggy. "Did you say the nursery was free?"

Though I rarely have problems making friends, I felt a little nervous and awkward, entering the doorway for that first luncheon. *What if I don't fit in?* I worried. The ambience didn't help.

The air had a bit of Cinderella magic to it when I stepped onto the gray and white marble floor of the grand foyer. The room was accented with gold crown moldings and massive bouquets of greenery and flowers. Mackey and I shared a nice life, but we were down-to-earth folks, not upper crust club members. I heard the low din of female chatter and laughter, before Peggy and I turned the corner and entered a meeting room filled with round tables covered by linen tablecloths, fine china, quality silverware, and crystal water glasses. My nerves ratcheted up a notch. Peggy must have noticed the tension in my body, because she laid a comforting hand on my arm.

I exhaled pent-up air when a kind woman sitting at a table with rows of nametags addressed me. Her light brunette perm bounced as she spoke. "Hi. Is this your first time attending?"

"Yes," I said with unnatural shyness.

"Welcome then. We're so glad you came. Did you have reservations?" the woman said.

The warm sparkle in her mocha brown eyes made me relax, even though I didn't know the answer to her question.

Peggy came to the rescue. "Yes, I made reservations for both of us."

"Perfect. What are your names so I can mark you off the list and give you your tags?" The woman fanned her hand to highlight the choices on the table.

"I'm Peggy and this is my friend, Linda."

The woman checked our names off her list, then searched out our tags. After Peggy secured hers onto her fuschia pink dress, she pinned my tag on the lapel of my shoulder-padded jacket, covered in yellow daisies. Then Peggy and I were escorted by another woman to a table near the podium at the front of the room.

Several women came and introduced themselves to me, until a clink, clink, clink on one of the crystal glasses signaled time to start. During the brief welcome speech, wait staff discreetly appeared with salads in hand. They were dressed impeccably in black and white.

After I finished my salad, the wait staff again showed up at the table, deftly removed the used plate, then slid a replacement in its place. A chicken breast smothered in cream sauce, roasted asparagus, mashed potatoes with chicken gravy, and a homemade yeast roll covered the generous dinner plate. The meal looked and smelled scrumptious.

Just as the cherry jubilee desserts were presented, the main speaker was introduced. Her message of hope and God's love, told through a fascinating story, touched my heart. But something else tickled my soul. I didn't understand exactly why or how I knew, but while the speaker talked, I felt in my gut that I was supposed to do what she was doing. I debated myself in my mind.

It's silly to think you could be a speaker.

But I feel so strongly that I should talk to someone and find out how you go about becoming one of their circuit speakers.

What do you have to say that anyone else would want to hear?

I think this is something God wants me to do.

How do you know it's God's voice you're hearing and not your own?

Lord, if this is You and not me, then show me the way to follow Your will. However, if my ego is somehow trying to convince me to do something You are not behind, shut any doors and don't let me pry them open.

After I prayed, I felt like it first made the most sense to get involved with the movers and shakers in the organization and find out how I could support them. I volunteered to help with the monthly meetings, jumped in with both feet to serve wherever I was needed, and true to my usual style, made some lifelong friends in the process. I also found out how to become a circuit speaker.

I attended the organization's speaker training, then prepared a story about my faith journey and recorded it on a cassette tape. (I understand. You may not know what a cassette tape is, or you haven't seen one in a really long time.) After that, for more than sixteen years, I was privileged to see God use my story as I shared His lovingkindness to me.

I'm still surprised at how powerfully God uses plain stories such as mine to save and strengthen anyone who believes that Christ died to set them free. Through the years, God's provision in obscure ways and the obvious, have allowed me the privilege of sharing His good news. And one trip really stands out in my mind.

I was scheduled to speak in a rural town northeast of Atlanta, Georgia. By then I'd become an experienced messenger, though God again needed to remind me that He is in control, and I am not. Just a week prior to that engagement, I faced a seemingly insurmountable problem, because of an outbreak of chickenpox. Three of my children were donning polka dots on their faces and bodies. I needed childcare, or I would be forced to cancel my speaking commitment last minute.

After stressing, then praying about my next course of action, I remembered my friend Peggy had moved to the area I was slated to speak. I called her and she agreed to rescue me, with an offer to babysit my three children at the venue location near her home while I spoke.

The morning of the luncheon, I started packing extra early for all four of us. I loaded up my minivan with car seats, toys, a diaper bag, baby food, Calamine lotion, traveling snacks, and my three kiddos. At that time, I was also a homeschooling mom (I know, overachiever), so there were also lesson plans, books, pencils, and backpacks to include. Plus, I needed my speaking notes, dressy clothes, and since it was 1990, I also had to take a map. (Remember that folded brochure with detailed traveling directions printed on paper, widely used prior to today's GPS?)

I met Peggy at a restaurant and nursed my baby while we caught up. When my wee one finished and was swaddled comfortably in her seat with Peggy's oversight, I headed for the van. I had to transform from "nursing mommy in a sweatsuit" to "speaker in professional wear."

When I opened my van door and reached for the travel hanger containing my dress, there was nothing there. Searching my mind in panic, I soon realized what I'd done. When I got home, I'd find my dress bag hanging neatly over the back of my sofa.

I looked down, scanning myself in dismay. This was the era of glittered sweatsuits, but the one I was wearing didn't have a bit of bling on it. If you wanted a gym workout, my suit fit the occasion, but speaking to a crowded women's luncheon? I feared I might pass out.

I tried to compose myself and returned to Peggy, empty-handed and in shock. My friend rescued me again.

"I've got one dress that's nice enough, and you are welcome to borrow it. I'm pretty sure it will fit you."

Five minutes later, after wrangling the kids into the van, I tailed Peggy as we drove to her house. Like my friends in

New Orleans would say, "I rode her bumper like red beans on rice."

The children must have recognized my elevated stress level. They remained unusually quiet in the backseat until my eight-year-old son broke the silence. He tried to comfort me with some words of wisdom.

"Mom," he said, "if God wants you to speak in a sweatsuit, you'll speak in a sweatsuit. If He wants you to speak in a dress, you'll speak in a dress."

Wow! Where did he get that kind of faith? I sure needed my son's dose of trusting confidence. In that stress-filled, panic-driven moment, God used the faith of an eight-year-old to encourage me with a simple truth—God is always in control, and He does provide. We just don't open our eyes to see His handiwork, sometimes. But this would not be my only reminder that day.

When we arrived at Peggy's house, I asked the kids to remain in the van while Peggy and I solved my dress dilemma. Their extraordinary compliance made me pause to thank my children, then I ran inside with my friend.

Peggy's dress was tightly waded up in her dryer, but at least it wasn't in her washing machine. I stripped off my sweaty sweatsuit and prayed, while waiting for her to quickly iron the dress, a mini-print. Feeling exposed and vulnerable, I stood in her living room in my slip, stockings, and shoes.

In only a couple of minutes, Peggy slipped the dress over my head. We flew out the door and back to the van, where she jumped into the driver's seat. Off to the venue we sped.

In spite of our best efforts, we arrived very late. In these settings, the luncheon started with a featured musician or special interest presentation. On this day, the last notes of two songs had already floated away when I walked in the door, got my speaker nametag from the check-in hostess, and discreetly took my place at the head table. I made it just in time for the main prize drawing.

It wasn't possible for the chairwoman to know the events of my last hour. And when I slipped in, she was distracted by reviewing the luncheon agenda and hadn't spotted me. Her choice for the prize-winning eligibility surprised me. The woman held up a cute gift bag and offered it to anyone wearing a mini-print dress.

A flurry of voices and activity instantly took over the room as women assessed each other and discussed their wardrobe decisions. As it turned out, however, I was the only woman in the room donning a mini-print dress. Feeling awkward, but urged by the ladies sitting at my table, I walked forward and introduced myself to the chairwoman.

When she saw my speaker tag, a look of relief washed over her face. I'm sure she'd fretted internally, thinking she might have to step in with an off-the-cuff message. The chairwoman insisted that I take the prize, and as I accepted it, I realized I had a free thank-you gift for Peggy. It made me happy, since she was the unspoken hero whom God used to save my day.

I'd barely sat down when the chairwoman read my introduction. It was my turn to take the mic, but I did not speak as planned. Instead, I wove the details of my day's events with my faith story, and they fit beautifully. My earlier embarrassment turned to joy as I told the women how God worked His ultimate plan in perfect fashion (pun intended). After all, He had just hand-selected my dress for this occasion.

At the conclusion of the event, a line of women waited to tell me how my story touched them. Many were especially impressed that I would confess my mistake, and said it was inspiring to hear me speak so openly and vulnerably. Others were floored by my son's demonstration of faith and mentioned feeling renewed trust in God from his confident decree.

I can only assume that the mini-print dress I wore, and the story of its role in my presentation that day, fulfilled God's purposes. Obviously, someone there needed to see Him as Jehovah Jireh, *my provider*. But I also hope my transparency gave others permission to consider how the stories of their mistakes and mess ups might provide just the faith boost another person needs to hear. When we are open to sharing the crazy peace God gives us, we pass it on, even in the midst of a crawfish hunt.

Opening Our Eyes

1. Do you stop to consider how God even provides your clothes? How can what we wear demonstrate our commitment to faith? *And why are you worried about clothing? Notice how the lilies of the field grow; they do not labor nor do they spin thread for cloth* (Matthew 6:28).

2. Have you ever felt panicked about needing something, only to have God provide at the last minute? Can you remember a time when you asked Him what you should wear? *Consider the lilies, how they grow: they neither labor nor spin; but I tell you, not even Solomon in all his glory clothed himself like one of these* (Luke 12:27).

CHAPTER ELEVEN

Crawfish Hunter

Sign on restaurant: *Crawfish are almost here!*

If you've never lived in Louisiana, you might not understand the faux pas of my chapter title. You may ask, how is it even possible to spin a tale regarding a hunter of crustaceans? Trust me, hunted they are not.

Crawfish, crayfish, crawdads, or mudbugs? Whatever you call them, these small, lobster look-alikes thrive in muddy Louisiana bayous. Between January through July, depending on the weather, they scoot in and out from under rocks in abundance.

Crawfish are trapped in nets or trap boxes, with just about any type of food source dangling inside. They will eat fish, other crawfish, vegetables, and aquatic plant life—there's little these omnivores won't consume. They naively swim into the net or box for a tasty morsel and exit as someone else's delicious bite.

The eating habits, or the way crawfish are caught, doesn't really matter to those of us who love them—just boil 'em up. My grandma always said, "I don't care what you call me, just don't call me late for dinner, especially when it comes to a spicy crawfish boil."

I agree with Grandma.

Since crawfish are mud dwellers, every Cajun cook knows you need to purge them in saltwater to make them edible. Once purged, load your favorite spices into boiling water, followed by your favorite vegetables. I've used various options, such as corn, potatoes, onions, garlic, broccoli, and lemons or oranges. I can almost smell the yummy aroma as I type. And crawfish always make me think of my brother.

Donald was quite the character. Typical is not a description anyone who knew him would use. He was good at anything he put his hand to and could rig whatever was necessary to get a job done—he took after our dad in every way. Not only was my brother a top-notch auto mechanic, but he was also a self-taught, modern-day Renaissance man. However, none of these traits would have made you think crawfish hunter. I'll never forget when Donald told me this hilarious tale.

Preparing for another one of his famous crawfish boils, Donald ingenuously decided to utilize his daughters' plastic kiddie pool for the overnight saltwater purge. Since he had three energetic dogs, he knew he needed a fail-proof spot to set everything up. After all, who wants their guests showing up for a crawfish boil without crawfish? So Donald placed the kiddie pool atop his picnic table, safely out of the dogs' reach.

The next morning, my brother went to the backyard to check on the crawfish purge. He did not find what he expected.

The kiddie pool lay upside down on top of the grass below the picnic table. Somehow, it had overturned. Lifting the pool up and inspecting the ground beneath, Donald saw dozens of his former prisoners escaping as fast as their ten, tiny, lobster-like legs could carry them. "Connie!" Donald yelled for his wife.

My sister-in-law dashed out the back door, the distress in Donald's voice alerting her to a crisis of some sort. She ran even faster when she saw Donald on all fours near the ground. If I'd witnessed that sight, I would have feared the worst too.

This began what is probably the only crawfish "hunt" in history.

Donald and Connie combed hundreds of green blades, frantically chasing crawfish for nearly an hour. Of course, not all were found. The missing escaped to who knows where.

Later, Donald recounted every detail of the uproarious story while we ate the unfortunate crawfish re-captives. Our bellies hurt from laughter. After my brother explained how the dogs could not have overturned the pool, someone asked Donald a question that started us off on a fun game.

"Just how did those little bugs do it? I know they're nocturnal, so it makes sense that they would wait for the cover of night, but just how did they make their great escape?"

This was the kind of questioning that made my big imagination soar. I started us off. "I'll bet there was an appointed leader who called them to order. I imagine they called him 'Coach Bug.' He probably climbed on the backs of some of his buddies until he could reach the lip of the pool. Then he peered over the edge, first on one side, then moved to another and another, so he could determine which was hanging closest to the table's edge."

Someone else in our group caught my vision and chimed in. "He knew the best tactic for the win would be to work as a unified team. So Coach Bug whistled for attention, then gave the troops a motivational speech that would make Vince Lombardi proud. He had to get everyone to buy into his game plan. He probably said something like, 'Okay guys, we have to remain united tonight. I've assessed the situation from both sides, and it clearly benefits us if we move to the left of the pool as one.'"

Donald picked up the story from there. "Yeah, he would have said, 'Using all of our weight is our best chance to escape. When I give the signal, we'll all shift to the left together, and I do mean everyone! Do any of you know which way is left? But the silence was deafening.'"

The voice Donald used in mimicking the crawfish leader made me hold my stomach with even more laughter.

Donald continued with his version of crawfish events. "I imagine they all looked at him like he was crazy at first. Individually, none of them weighed much. But the indomitable spirit of their leader was contagious. 'Come on, team, together we are a formidable force. We can do this!'

"Believing him, the troops crawled, climbed, shoved, slid, and climbed some more, scrunching in unity, for the cause. And don't think there weren't sacrifices. While some were stepping on heads to move to the top, they poked out a few eyes along the way. Others had their armor, also known as their crustacean shells, damaged. But . . ." Donald drew the last word out and paused, waiting for one of us to take over.

When no one else seized the opportunity, I obliged. "But even though the crawfish captives sustained losses along the way, they ultimately achieved victory. Coach Bug urged them in the charge as some on the bottom took a running leap at the bunched up group, causing the pool to tilt. 'That's it, boys,' he shouted. 'Do it again! Heave, ho, heave ho.'

"The pool began to rock, slightly at first, but with each jump on the pile, it angled further downward. Finally, the redistributed weight of the group did its job, the plastic pool toppled to the ground with a thud. They were free."

My sister-in-law, Connie, closed the story. "Coach Bug told his people, 'Bravo, guys. Always remember, no matter how stuck you feel, you don't have to go it alone. We're in it together doesn't have to be a cliché. When we take it to heart, and ask others for help, we usually find a way out of whatever is holding us back.'"

I'm pretty sure our whole group oohed and awed over Connie's addition of the inspirational insight at the end. But we did so, because we recognized its truth. God's crazy peace is always available, and He almost always provides it through His people.

Donald and Connie's "crawfish hunter" escapades provided much entertainment many times over. It was repeatedly regaled through the years. But as in most stories, there is also a lesson hidden inside the parable.

Today whenever I head to a crawfish boil, I am reminded that God is the perfect strategic leader. He knows there is strength in numbers, and He surrounds us with reinforcements all of the time. But we often remain stuck, because we don't listen to His instructions and refuse the help He provides. Without realizing it, we exchange crazy chaos for His crazy peace.

I've often wondered what happened to the crawfish Donald and Connie didn't find that day. Did they wander into other unknown dangers? Did some of them join forces and truly find a way out? How many of them picked up the scent of the bayou and trekked toward home? I'll never know those answers, but I do know this: I don't own a crawfish net, but I have a pool net. So if any stray crawfish come my way, well, "Bon Appetit." I'll get the spices, honey, you put the pot on to boil.

It's good to laugh and it's good to learn. Sometimes, we can even find joy in the drama.

Opening Our Eyes

1. When have reinforcements helped you work toward a greater good? Have you ever joined hands, feet, and hearts with a group to lift others up? *Make my joy complete by being of the same mind, maintaining the same love, united in spirit, intent on one purpose. Do nothing from selfishness or empty conceit, but with humility consider one another as more important than yourselves; do not merely look out for your own personal interests, but also for the interest of others* (Philippians 2:2–4).

2. When was the last time you laughed with people you care about? Do you see God in the silly as well as the serious? *There is an appointed time for everything. And there is a time for every matter under heaven* (Ecclesiastes 3:1).

CHAPTER TWELVE

Experiencing the Drama of God

I was minding my own business, then God called me to mind HIS!

In my younger years, I was guilty of wrapping God up tightly in a little mental box I kept in my mind. However, I soon realized He can never be fully understood—His power is much too mighty to be crammed into anyone's box. Only through experiencing Him have I learned that His Holy Spirit cannot be contained, but it can be spread abroad to others. And He often uses us to help roll out His holy plans.

I heard/felt God speaking to my heart, but at first, I wasn't sure if it was His voice or mine. Was this something He wanted me to do, or was it an inner desire I'd been unaware of, disguised as His? I began to ask for confirmation, struggling to believe what I was being told. Repeatedly, the tug at my heart and mind shocked me, both in strength and nature. I had zero training, no experience, and the call felt quite outside the parameters of my comfort zone. Where was this coming from?

Little did I know at the time that this was exactly where God wanted me to be, uncomfortable and dependent upon Him. He was pushing me to live completely in His spiritual zone. I was about to experience the drama of God like never before.

For three years, my children participated in a Christian musical theater troupe, and they became addicted to the drama scene. Then Mac's company relocated us from North Carolina to Atlanta. Shortly after we arrived, the kids urged me to find a local theater troupe and sign them up. But I found no such ministry opportunity. This is where God's idea met my uncertainty.

The need for a Christian-based musical theatre in the Atlanta area seemed obvious to me. Thank goodness when God calls, He wisely reveals only the pertinent information needed at the time. I might have opted out if I'd known just how far this thing would go. But I couldn't shake the incessant tug.

I turned to my piano-tuning friend, Rick, who had a ministry to Russian believers. I wondered how he knew where to start. Maybe he could guide me as to what to do first. After all, where does one begin when God calls you to something incredibly bigger than yourself?

When he finished making my 1901 antique upright sound melodious, he swiveled on the piano bench until he faced me.

I got straight to the point. "How do you know where to start when God whispers a call to your heart?"

Rick suggested I stop at a little church on Highway 41 that performed locally written productions around town.

I was shocked and then stammered, "Wait!" as I headed to the kitchen. I returned with my manilla folder and flipped it open to show Rick a single piece of folded loose-leaf paper on which was the name and number of the church!

"I recently drove past that church and their theatrical marquee caught my eye. So, I wrote the name and number down." *Confirmation number one.*

The next day was the monthly Homeschool Skate Day. As I turned left into the parking lot toward the rink, I had to do a double-take because I saw the very same make-shift church building on my right that I had noticed the day before. *Confirmation number two.*

My three anxious skaters quickly exited the van and raced for the front door of the rink. I got them settled, then slowly drove my van toward the little church I felt compelled to visit.

I knocked at the sliding glass door and swallowed hard. A man of average height and build slid the door open and introduced himself as the pastor. "Can I help you?" he asked, welcoming me into his office.

I awkwardly attempted to spurt out my reason for the visit. "I feel like God is calling me to start a children's musical theatre troupe like the one we enjoyed in North Carolina." I told him that I had mentioned this to a few friends in my homeschool co-op and they sounded interested, but "I'm not sure what to do next with this call."

Over the next hour, we discussed details, the fascinating and the practical. The pastor told me how he ended up at the church when I arrived, opening the door to my knock, when as a lay pastor who held a day job, he was rarely in the building at that time of day. But his wife delivered their baby the night before, so before going home to sleep, he "just happened" to stop in and check the church's answering machine. *Confirmation number three.*

Finally, the pastor smiled. "Well, it sounds like you have the ministry and I have the building. All we need to do is decide the best day of the week for your soon-to-be-born theater troupe to meet." Before I left, the pastor gave me the key to his church. *Confirmation number four.*

Though I'd received multiple confirmations that this was God's plan, I still felt inadequate. I could only follow

God's direction, the opportunities set before me, and my gut based on limited experience as a "drama mama."

I planned the first official parents' meeting by preparing my thoughts and buying some refreshments. I set out a few costumes and scrapbooks from my children's previous productions at the church for added inspiration. That's all I knew to do.

Thunderclouds accumulated throughout the day of our scheduled gathering. By evening, the heavy deluge of rain made seeing to drive difficult. I felt a bit discouraged when only three other families attended the meeting, yet God encouraged my heart. Before I fell asleep later that night, in my spirit I heard the words, *I will rain children down on you.* It was enough to propel me forward.

I scheduled our premiere theater class purely by faith. This was to be musical theater, after all, and I didn't play an instrument, nor could I read music at all. But God provided. A woman named Dianna called me the night before our first session to ask if her daughter could attend. Then as an aside, she said, "Oh, and by the way, I teach voice and piano." *Confirmation number five.*

Attempting to follow God's guidance as I felt instructed, with just my three children and seven others, we started holding classes in September. Word spread swiftly through the home-schooling community, and children soon began to trickle into our program. By January, we finally had forty children, enough to cast our first production for May.

God brought forth many people with various needed giftings to help. I was thankful, as I had none. Our troupe was blessed by talents from those who knew everything from lighting to keyboard to costumes. We even received backing from a financial "angel" who filled my Honda Accord to the ceiling with costumes more than once.

In the second year, seventy children signed up. God rained down the children as He promised.

For a total of ten years, until my husband's job transferred us to another state, I experienced God's supply through this adventure. Then I handed the program over to a team of women who had been faithful in using their gifts for this supernatural work of the Lord. The transfer included more than 1,200 costume pieces, props, sets, and lighting equipment we had accumulated, which previously overflowed my basement. This led to the rental of a storage unit.

Today this organization is still in existence. As of this writing, it has expanded greatly, utilizing the call of many who have stepped forth with their gifts, to faithfully continue the work for another seventeen years.

In addition to myself, the volunteers who labored with me, as well as those I've never met, have been privy to the workings of our God through the musical theater troupe. We've witnessed His many provisions and seen the fulfillment of His extraordinary plans. I personally know that whatever God calls into existence, He always provides, performs, and produces by His bountiful hand and not our own. That knowledge gives me ongoing crazy peace.

At that time in my life, I was nothing more than a facilitator and servant for those God gathered. He faithfully brought a too-numerous-to-count number of children through the program, who were not only trained in music but also in their faith. It blessed me beyond my ability to truly explain, to play a small role in God's will as it was done.

So let me ask you. Are you experiencing God as He works in your life and through your hands and abilities? He still desires to use His people, so He can accomplish His great and mighty plans and further His kingdom. If your answer is not yet, step up to the plate, and say, "Yes Lord. Use me in whatever way You desire. I am willing." Then get ready, for He still speaks today—although sometimes, it's Greek to me.

Opening Our Eyes

1. Have you ever felt convicted about following through on an everyday task that you would have preferred to avoid? Do you recall a time where putting in the work on a smaller project led to an opportunity to do something bigger? *The one who is faithful in a very little thing is also faithful in much. . .* (Luke 16:10a).

2. When was the last time you felt God nudging you beyond your comfort zone? Name something God has done that was exceedingly and abundantly beyond all that you asked, thought, dreamed, or hoped. *Now to Him who is able to do far more abundantly beyond all that we ask or think, according to the power that works within us* (Ephesians 3:20).

CHAPTER THIRTEEN

It's All Greek to Me

What is a foreign language? Actually, all languages are foreign to me. I speak one language and one language only (with a heavy New Orleans accent), and I'm still working on how to improve my English. I can study to enhance my vocabulary, but there's not really a lot of hope regarding my accent. You can imagine my surprise when God chose to use me in a translation situation—it started out altogether foreign to me.

Stop for just a moment, take a breath, and think about it. How powerful is the Creator of all? My brain cannot contain the enormity of His magnificent presence. He spoke, and the world was flung into space. Then He spoke again, transforming the darkness by light.

God is able to transform, inform, and conform our hearts, minds, souls, and bodies. None of us can really take credit for what we have ever created, invented, perfected, or altered. All creativity remains within Him and Him alone. Anything that man will ever bring about ultimately originated from God. All good gifts come from above, as does our ability to create.

I want my eyes to always recognize God's work, and His guiding hand in everyday events. He has shown His powerful self to me through innumerable ways and stages throughout my life. But for some reason, I don't always slow down enough to realize that He continues to show up in my world, just as He did to the first church long ago.

The Bible tells us that in the early church, tongues of fire came down upon the people, so they could understand and believe the words of truth spoken to them. Now, I have never seen a fiery tongue, and my guess is that you probably haven't either, but God did allow me to witness His might and power by opening the ears and heart of a lady from Greece.

It started when I attended a seminar in Florida where I learned how to share the gospel with young children using nothing more than our two hands. I learned to show each word in 1 Corinthians 15:3–4 using motions, because this verse contains the entire gospel in a nutshell. Little did I know that this simple lesson meant to bring understanding to children would also equip me to reach a woman from a country far, far away. The opportunity presented itself within minutes of landing at home. God never wastes a thing.

I stood in the aisle waiting to deplane in New Orleans when I overheard two flight attendants discussing a problem. One held a piece of paper with a phone number written on it. From the conversation I quickly deduced that it belonged to a Greek-speaking woman who understood no English. She needed someone to call her sister with news that she had just arrived.

The problem-solver in me rose up. I am always trying to fix the world, so this type of thing happens to me on a regular basis. I excused myself and stepped right into the middle of their conversation. My mama would do the same, so I come by it legitimately.

I told the attendants that I would make the call for the woman, while simultaneously providing instructive motioning for her to follow me. Prior to the time of a cell phone in every pocket or purse, airports had rows of pay phones banked along the walls inside of terminals. I walked up to the first empty one I saw, with my new Greek friend in tow, and dialed the number scrawled on the paper.

A pleasant-sounding woman answered on the second ring. "Hello," she said.

"Hi, I have your sister with me at the airport," I blurted without thinking about how that might sound.

Thankfully, the woman was unperturbed. "Oh, thank you," she said. "I can come pick her up. Where are you?"

"We can meet you outside the terminal near baggage claim if you like."

"I'll leave right now," she said, then hung up. Neither one of us thought to make sure I had her vehicle description.

I lead my Greek friend to baggage and managed to help her pull her luggage off the conveyor belt. Once we both had our bags in hand, we walked outside where I motioned for her to join me on a bench.

It seemed futile to even attempt a conversation, but ever the optimist and burdened with compassion for her, I felt compelled to persevere. By absolute faith, I asked the woman the most important question anyone will ever hear. "Do you know Jesus Christ?"

I waited for her response but got none.

"Do you know of God?" I tried again.

There was still no change in her demeanor or countenance.

Appearing not to understand a single word I said, my mind spun into action. *This is exactly the type of situation where putting into action what I learned at the seminar makes total sense. Maybe I've traveled and studied for such a time as this!*

I began using my hands to share the gospel, telling her, "Christ died for our sins." I thought I saw a flicker of

111

response, so I motioned more. "1 Corinthians 15:3–4 says He was buried and raised on the third day."

Suddenly, to my shock, she began to cry.

I thought, *Whoa God, you did it. You spoke to her heart in spite of our language barriers.*

On that day, I believe God translated His Word right there on the airport bench in New Orleans. He had equipped me to sign and softened this woman's heart, opening her understanding with His message of love. Now, that's good news!

In our crazy busy culture, we can miss out on crazy peace if we aren't careful. We forget that God Almighty is still in the miracle business. He has not lost the ability to heal blind eyes and awaken deaf ears. He will even save people from death when it isn't time for Him to take them home. So surely translating languages cannot be a problem for our awesome Creator.

More than ever, we would benefit from tapping into the power of God, who can bring the world closer together, ministering to people as each one has need. God can do whatever He wants whenever He wants. He is always at work to serve His greater purpose, which is to love the world and draw all nations, tribes, and tongues to Himself. He never sleeps, is everywhere at once, and will use whatever means He deems necessary to reach souls, one at a time, day after day. This makes me wonder why we are amazed when we witness Him in action.

That day so long ago, I received a tremendous blessing because God had prepared me as His servant. I was in the right place at the right time—but that wasn't enough. I had to stand ready to go to work for Him when opportunity presented itself. I had to say yes. The same is true for you. If you want to experience unimaginable blessings, you must look for opportunity and say yes too. Are you ready?

Join me in asking for an open heart and open eyes to see God's work around us. Then be willing to step out by faith and be used by Him. It's a marvelous thing to be used of the Lord, even when it takes years for the purpose to be revealed.

Opening Our Eyes

1. If you only had one opportunity to tell someone about Jesus, how would you go about it? Who have you not shared the good news of the gospel with that you feel compelled to? . . . *that Christ died for our sins, according to the Scriptures, and that He was buried, and that He was raised on the third day according to the Scriptures* (1 Corinthians 15:3–4).

2. Have you ever faced a seemingly impossible situation, only to experience a miraculous outcome? What is the greatest thing God has ever brought you through? *Is there anything too difficult for the Lord?* (Genesis 18:14a).

CHAPTER FOURTEEN

Misplaced Lace

My honey and I finally made it to the altar after dating for seven and a half years. The wedding was perfect. Fresh flowers graced the air with their subtle perfume. The soft rustle of my lacy white dress made me feel like a princess. My tuxedo-decked prince charming stood at the front of the church, smiling with anticipation while I made my way up the aisle. When I felt the strength of his hand as it wrapped around mine, I couldn't imagine anything but our bright future together.

We vowed before God and man to willingly leave our families and cleave to one another.

The only history I had regarding marriage was the life modeled by my dad and my father-in-law. They both spent their entire lives settled in one city, so I always figured marriage meant staying rooted. I was wrong. The very next morning after our wedding, we flew from New Orleans, Louisiana, to Schenectady, New York.

By marrying Mackey, I soon discovered moss doesn't grow under the feet of a nuclear field engineer, nor the feet of his wife. For our entire married life "Mr. General Electric" decided where we lived and for how long. But the saga of constant packing and moving and relocating was a shared responsibility, and it began on our first day as husband and wife. Surprisingly, I loved assimilating into new homes, communities, and social circles. I remember one particular day as I prepared us for relocation to yet another new address.

I carefully climbed the attic staircase with plans to clean out and organize, so the packers and movers could get to work. Dust stirred as I pulled stacks from corners and opened containers to review the contents. Then I spotted a large empty box that made my eyes mist. I hadn't seen it since we moved into this house.

I lifted the box from its perch on top of other important mementos, surprised at how light it felt, then sat on the edge of a nearby trunk. I laid the box on my lap and gingerly raised the lid's corner and pulled back. What I saw took my breath away. Or maybe I should say more accurately, what I didn't see caused me to stop breathing.

The box was empty. But how could I have misplaced the contents of this box? There was no mistaking though, my wedding dress box, circa 1974, lay barren before me.

After the first wave of shock came and went, I calmed down and told myself, *Think, Linda, think! Where did you last see the dress? And why didn't you write your name in it, so if it got lost someone would know who to return it to?*

In moments of panic, we often don't think logically. It didn't occur to me that as a mom who has printed children's names in many a coat, there was no reason I would have written my name in my wedding dress. After all, who does that? Not me, or anyone I'm aware of for that matter.

Running through all the possible options for the whereabouts of my wedding dress, I tried to remain calm. *Could I have left it at a dry cleaner? I think they only hold items for thirty days. Please God, don't let them have thrown my dress away. Please let it turn up in good condition.*

I racked my brain some more. *Maybe I gave it to a friend for safekeeping.* But after running through a list of friends in my head, I came to a single conclusion. *Nope, I'm sure I didn't do that.* Then a memory popped into my mind. *The last time I remember seeing it was in 1984 when I wore it in that bridal fashion show.*

After I'd spent way too much emotion I finally gave up the stressful battle in my mind and cried out to God, "Lord, I only want this dress so I can hand it, or even a piece of lace from it, to my baby girl on her wedding day. I know

You know where the dress is, and I know You can keep it protected until the right time."

After I'd prayed, that familiar crazy peace only God can give came over me. It enabled me to release all the worry, frustration, and fear that had gripped me only minutes earlier. Having read Scripture, I knew I could trust God with that surrender, knowing He cares about the things I care about, because He cares for me. But I did have doubts that He would waste His time on my latest blunder—after all, didn't my Heavenly Father have more important things to attend to? I decided to accept my lot and move on with the packing.

I soon found it easier to put the wedding gown out of my mind as life shifted back into busy mode. We went through two more relocations and reveled in the birth of our fourth child. For the next few years I homeschooled and carted kids to their way-too-many extracurricular activities. In all of it, I enjoyed being a wife and mom.

Occasionally, I thought about the missing dress and wondered about the mystery of it all, but I did so stressless and filled with the crazy peace I felt God gave to me. As a woman of faith I truly believed that if God felt I needed the garment He would bring it to me. It would take twenty years and seven months before I finally discovered what happened to my dress. And even then it was my husband and not me who found it.

Mac joined his siblings in New Orleans so they could clean out their parents' home in preparation for his dad's move into an assisted living facility. I was quite surprised when Mackey called with what I considered a ridiculous question. "What does your wedding dress look like?"

All I could think was: *Really? Weren't you there with me at the altar that day?* But instead of voicing my frustration, I calmly described the dress as best I could from memory.

"Well, guess what," Mac's tone, almost always quiet and matter of fact in his engineer kind of way, had a little extra energy to it. "I think I found it."

"You found my wedding dress? Where?"

"In Dad and Mom's attic. We were going through their belongings, and we found a box just mixed with everything else. The dress was inside."

"What was it doing in their attic? And how in the world did it get there?"

Neither one of us had any idea. It made no sense. When we made our annual Christmas trip home to New Orleans, our van was always loaded down with three kids and gifts. We had no extra room for something like a bulky wedding dress box. I could think of no reason anyone else would have taken it, and I couldn't imagine my having done so without recollecting the movement of something I held so dear. The last place I knew I had it was when I wore it in a fashion show, but that took place in Georgia, not Louisiana.

When Mac returned home, he carried the lacy dress inside and handed it to me for close inspection. It was definitely mine. I remembered back to my prayer twenty years earlier when I'd asked God to let it turn up. It might have taken a couple of decades, but He delivered. I began to thank God for answering me in such a concrete way.

Maybe one day when I'm in heaven I'll hear the answer to the mystery of how my wedding dress moved from my attic to my in-laws'. As ridiculous as this story may seem to some though, there are significant lessons hiding within.

First, even when a prayer seems pretty unimportant to others our concerns matter to God. He does care about the little things in life which are precious to us.

Second, whatever else I had been praying for, even when the years slipped by without an obvious answer, God didn't forget, and He did not fall asleep. Ever. We may stop praying, but God doesn't stop moving. He *is* always working, and He *will* bring to pass what appears impossible, according to *His* will. But only when HE says the timing is right.

In 2015, we planned not one, but two weddings as both our daughters were getting married. Sometime later, I asked Mac to get that mysterious box, complete with the dress inside, from our attic. I had told God I wanted to pass down a piece of lace to my daughter for her wedding.

Each of the girls tried my dress on and even took photos of themselves in it, but neither one chose to wear the gown for their big day. Instead, we cut the lace cuffs off, complete with snaps, and wrapped them around their lovely bouquet stems. It ended up being a sweet touch.

After both weddings were over, I wondered what to do with that box filled with lace and organza. I asked God for wisdom and guidance.

Two years later, my answer came clear and strong while reading an article about a ministry in McDonough, Georgia. *Rachel's Gift* takes donated wedding dresses and their volunteer seamstresses transform them into burial gowns for infants who pass away in the NICU. Thinking about the grieving families of those sweet babies made my decision easy. I packed up that forty-one-year-old dress and mailed it off to Georgia. What a blessing to know that it continues to fulfill an even better purpose.

The Bible tells us not to lay up any treasures on earth. Instead of fretting over possessions that do not have eternal value, we can place our hope in the Father's plans. Even if we experience loss we can trust God's answers. And when His timing does not align with our desires, we can rest in the assurance that ultimately the outcome will bring Him glory. Sometimes, we must simply exercise a nutty kind of faith.

Opening Our Eyes

1. Have you ever imagined what beautiful sights heaven will hold for us? Is there any possession you feel convicted to release to Christ? *That of everything that He has given Me I will lose nothing, but will raise it up on the last day* (John 6:39b).

2. What have you lost that threw you into an emotional tailspin? Have you ever given something you treasured away for a greater good? "*Do not store up for yourselves treasures on earth, where moth and rust destroy, and where thieves break in and steal. But store up for yourselves treasures in heaven, where neither moth nor rust destroys, and where thieves do not break in or steal; for where your treasure is, there your heart will be also*" (Matthew 6:19–21).

CHAPTER FIFTEEN

Nutty Kind of Faith

My husband, Mackey, was the strong silent type and a man of great faith. His testimonies of God's provision, or of hearing Him speak, always built my faith. The story that affected me most was when I learned that Jesus was even Lord of Mac's tool shed.

Our first starter home was nestled within a soft slope surrounded by wooded areas on three sides. We were flanked on the right by neighbors high atop a hill. This meant that during the fall, their foliage drifted down, down, down, totally covering the driveway and surrounding grassy area of our lot. In the south, lawn care can seem endless as summer slides into autumn.

Mac had finished the cleanup of our front and back yards and turned to the strip of property adjacent to our driveway, so he could add the final touches to our landscaping. His weed whacker buzzed across the last green blades when something metallic flew off. He watched it land somewhere in the great abyss of weeds, leaves, and brush he had piled up.

A close examination of the trimmer revealed that he'd lost an essential nut. Mackey patiently searched, pulling back strands of debris as he hunted. My husband searched long after others would have resigned. But as the sun began slipping away on its journey west, and darkness took over, his frustration finally piqued. The loss of daylight ended the nut hunt, so he gathered up the dead whacker and stashed it in the shed with his other tools until he could deal with it the next day.

Mac, being the frugal man that he was, called Sears for a replacement nut.

The person on the phone said, "I'm sorry, sir, but we no longer carry that specialty item."

Mac hung up feeling confused, but undeterred. His next option was to search for a similar part in his box of miscellaneous, odd-sized nuts and bolts. But he dug to no avail.

As the seasons changed, spring sprung again, and routine outdoor chores took priority once more. Mackey pulled out his tools, including the lame weed whacker, no longer able to ignore the "out of sight out of mind" trimmer. He laid it aside, focusing on the working tools at his disposal.

After mowing the front and back lawns, Mac was haunted by the colossal question of what to do about the side yard, which needed the smaller size and nimbleness of a trimmer. The thought of renewing his search for the missing nut felt daunting, but our newlywed checkbook said purchasing a new weed whacker was not really an option.

Sighing deeply, Mac faced the dreaded, much-weathered side yard. He analyzed the landscape which was overflowing with decomposed leaves, twigs, weeds, and compacted sludge coming from the hill up above. The lawn at that side of our house held a monumental mess of mush. But with no other recourse, Mac decided to make one last-ditch (pun intended) effort and renewed his search for the aberrant nut.

Facing the daunting impossibility of finding it on his own, Mackey turned to God in prayer. He then felt as if God was leading him to an obscure spot, in the midst of deepened mush. It seemed a little crazy to assume the tiny piece might actually be buried in that particular place, but Mac sensed his trust in God's direction would pay off. Much like the men of old mentioned in Hebrews 11, also known as the Hall of Faith chapter of the Bible, Mac resolved and took action.

With the kind of trust Noah must have exhibited when he built a boat prior to rain ever falling on the earth, Mackey walked. Showing the level of faith Abraham demonstrated when he packed his knife and some wood for a hike up the mountain with his son, Isaac, Mac put one foot in front of the other. Mirroring the degree of certainty required of Moses, as he stood between Egyptian chariots and the Red Sea before stepping onto the dry land God provided, Mac moved resolutely. Staring down doubt like Daniel when he was boxed in with a brood of lions, Mac came eye to eye with the mushy mess. And displaying the confidence of David, as he reached inside his pouch for that small, smooth stone, to target the formidable Goliath, Mac reached into the weedy spot.

It may seem odd to contrast my husband's actions that day to the familiar faithful of the Bible, but I believe the comparison is warranted. Because whether we need help locating a tiny object or are desperate for difference-making guidance on the biggest issue we've ever faced, God is waiting and willing to provide.

In truth, my husband had to follow the same steps as the biblical greats who came before him. Mackey had to listen to and believe that still, small voice, calling out to his soul. He had to obey, and step toward the area where he was directed. And he had to stoop down and put his hands into the thick, leafy muck, feeling around until he pinched something tangible. In a miraculous way only God could, Mac's fingers came into contact with that runaway nut.

Immediately, Mackey came rushing inside the house, holding that testimonial metallic piece up for me to see. He choked on his words. "Linda, look what God just did!" he said.

Still trying to register exactly what Mac was pinching so tightly between his fingers, I said, "What?"

"Look." My husband held the nut up close to my eyes, as if I were legally blind. "I found it. I found the trimmer nut. It's unbelievable. I prayed and asked God where it was, then I felt like I was supposed to check the side of the house one more time. It felt a little nutty to think I might have any chance at finding it, but then all the people in the Bible probably felt a little nutty sometimes too. Yet they didn't let that stop them from believing God—and look how things turned out for them. Now my nutty kind of faith has proven that even today He is still in the miracle business."

Mackey's crazy peace quickly became contagious for me. Awestruck over our everyday miracle, Mac and I rejoiced and worshipped all afternoon. This taught us early in our marriage to trust God with the small things as well as the massive. We realized that our great and mighty God is living inside of us, and He wants to lead us daily.

A little while later, Mackey tightened that nut on his lame weed whacker, saving us a bundle of money we didn't have to spend on a new trimmer. I wish we would've enshrined that nut as a symbol to ourselves and others, reminding us that the miraculous works of God are still available to us today.

Now, many years later, I still find it amazing that my man of nutty faith dared to believe his prayer would and could be answered. Although Mackey went home to heaven early in his life, his example still influences my own trust in our Heavenly Father.

God is Immanuel, meaning God with us. And nothing is impossible with Him, not even unearthing the location of a nut hidden in deep, mucky coverage—a year later. The Lord loves to show Himself strong through our weakness. He loves to remind us that He has a plan and a purpose for everything in our lives. He loves to show us He is with us through the tiniest details of life. He loves to hear us ask Him for help. He loves it when we dare to believe.

Never give in to the doubts that would tell you something is seemingly too insignificant for you to ask God about. Don't fear that your circumstance or situation is beyond prayer or God's ability to show you a way out of it. If it's important to you, it's important to Him.

Dare to ask Him. Dare to seek Him. Dare to believe Him. Dare to trust and obey God with any concern you carry. Let me challenge you with a series of life-altering questions.

- Have you ever trusted the Lord, really trusted Him, with your life?

- Have you ever prayed, truly expecting Him to answer your prayer?

- Have you ever asked Him to carry your impossible burden?

- Have you ever asked God to show Himself strong, to and through you?

May we ask God, the authority on, under, and above the earth, to stretch our faith. May we live our lives to glorify God, even in the most mundane of things, even if it's as small as a weed-whacking nut.

Stretch us, Lord. Heal our unbelief. Give us a nutty kind of faith. Fill our spirits with crazy peace and the sweet aroma of our Savior.

Opening Our Eyes

1. When, if ever, have you dared to thank God before
    you saw results of your faith-filled prayers? Is
    there any situation or circumstance that you have
    withheld from belief-wrapped prayer? *Now faith is the
    certainty of things hoped for, a proof of things not seen*
    (Hebrews 11:1).

2. What is the tiniest thing you have ever prayed for?
    How has God shown up and shown off in your
    everyday events? *And He said to them, "Because of your
    meager faith; for truly I say to you, if you have faith the
    size of a mustard seed, you will say to this mountain,
    'Move from here to there,' and it will move; and nothing
    will be impossible for you"* (Matthew 17:20).

CHAPTER SIXTEEN

Sweet Aroma
of the Savior

H as an aroma ever transported you to the memory of a particular person, place, or even an activity? Maybe a certain scent carried with it reminiscing thoughts of a loved one or merely a comforting remembrance. A simple, fragrant trace of odor, although invisible, is powerful enough to transcend decades.

In my case, God used the power of perfume to remind me of His lavish love at a time when my whole world had recently spun out of control. With fragrance, God stirred my heart and mind to focus on Him, reminding me that He was, is, and always will take care of me.

It wasn't how any of us expected things to turn out, least of all Mackey. Vacations are supposed to represent joy, laughter, and rest, not throw us into a fog of grief. The unexpected passing of my husband of forty-two years ended any thoughts of fun in the sun for our family. He died in one of those tragic, unforeseen moments, where his body suddenly gave out.

A few days after, I was blindsided by another secondary loss, albeit rooted in an insignificant private thought. *I will have to buy my own perfume.* I said it to no one but myself, and then I wept afresh, for a countless time.

But something about the incessant, private but painful inner voice's message struck a chord of intimacy inside me. Every time the reality of buying my own perfume hit again, I had another messy cry. Everyone who suffers loss will experience those personal moments, isolated, perhaps unique or maybe even silly to someone else, but oh so painful.

I had good reason for being affected so strongly by the scent of perfume. My honey always kept my favorite scents well-stocked so fragrance became a constant reminder that I had to learn to live without my Mackey and his loving ways. But in spite of my ongoing struggles, other loved ones helped compel me to live on.

Three weeks after Mackey's funeral, I traveled to Atlanta to visit my son, who faced a medical issue. Thankfully, all went well. I was soon on my way home where I could mourn my husband's death without concern of adding to the sorrow of my children.

On my drive back to Mississippi, I took a shortcut through Dallas, Georgia, to avoid Atlanta traffic. That's when I spotted a little thrift shop. The brightly colored baby equipment out front drew me inside, since only three months earlier I had earned my "Nana" status. A fresh pang of regret struck me as I glanced at the shop's sign. It read, *Grandpa and Me.*

Browsing around, I fondled many infant items, and held back tears as I reconsidered the fact that our new granddaughter would never know the amazing man she might have called "Pop Pop." Images of Mackey's delight, written in smiles and sparkling eyes when he held our new little love, blanketed my mind. His enthusiasm over our new grandparent's role had been understated, true to his character, yet obviously clear.

Eventually, I found some thank you notes I both needed and liked and paid for them. As I turned to leave, the shopkeeper called me back to her counter. I thought maybe I had paid her incorrectly, since after all, I was traipsing around in a fog of grief. She asked me to hand her my bag. What happened next, only God could've orchestrated.

The cashier tucked a small card with a sample vial of perfume into my bag. "I'm sorry, I almost forgot to give you your little gift," she said.

With no regard for pleasantries or etiquette, I immediately gasped for breath, turned, and made a quick exit. I knew an ugly cry was coming and its powerful wave would be too great to stop. After just three weeks, I'd already learned that deluges of tears are often uncontrollable. Not only are you unable to thwart the waves, but at times, you cannot foresee the triggers that set them off. Sure enough, sorrow flooded my heart and spilled over my cheeks before I even passed the exit sign.

When I got to my car, I sat for a short while, clutching the small paper bag with God's intimate gift inside. When I felt more composed and able, I took the perfume vial out and read the attached card. *Write your hurts in the sand but carve your blessings in stone.*

I read it a second time, then heard God's comforting voice speaking softly to my grieving soul. "I've got this, and I've got you. I will be your husband now."

I knew God's promise from the Bible to be a husband to the husbandless, but now it was personal, intimately personal. I sat stunned, crying another river of tears, intermingled with a little crazy peace. Thus, began my long emotional trip back home to Mississippi.

During that drive my spiritual life was strengthened in ways that can take years, apart from the depth of dramatic experiences. I felt overwhelmed at the thought that God cared enough to love and cherish me in a way previously held private between Mackey and me. Only God knew how much it meant that my husband picked out and provided my perfume.

The small gift of a fragrance sample made me feel cherished and treasured. It reminded me that all of God's promises are true, including His vow to never leave me. This thought encouraged me to press even closer to God and to depend upon Him for all things ahead in my new role as a widow. That crazy peace lingered—it still does today.

I continue to witness God's going before me in all things. He holds me securely, and He helps me move forward, one step at a time. Whenever I am slammed head-on with a wave of grief, He is there to help me catch my breath again. He has met my needs and more. The Lord faithfully steps into this realm of life, even using physical objects such as a vial of perfume, to lavish His love upon me. What crazy peace His love brings to my weary soul.

Time and again, God proved His name, Jehovah Jireh, meaning He is the ultimate provider, to Mac and me. But for the Lord to orchestrate every detail of that trip after Mackey's death felt like provision on steroids. He took care of the timing, my shortcut, the clerk's remembrance, and the perfume sample, all of the practical parts. But God also provided for my emotional needs. He will do the same for you.

I know it makes God happy when we brag on Him. He has empowered us to bring the sweet aroma of His goodness, His mercy, and His tender care, everywhere we go. He is the fragrance we need until we see Him face to face in all

His splendor and glory. And His scent, symbolized by the love we display, should trail behind our every encounter.

So the next time you inhale a trace of perfume, think of it as a reminder of the sweet aroma of God's intimate and cherishing love for you. Open His Word, sit at His feet, and let Him pour His lavish adoration over you, personally. Allow Him to empower you as a believer and conduit of His good news, spreading the pleasing fragrance of Christ, our Savior, wherever you go. If we let it, His powerful scent and crazy peace will follow us everywhere—even in the scary places. And it might, just might, follow us into the wild blue yonder.

Opening Our Eyes

1. Is there a particular symbol or scent that always reminds you of God's sweet care and provision? When have you experienced the pleasing aroma of Jesus Christ in an everyday event? *But thanks be to God, who always leads us in triumph in Christ, and through us reveals the fragrance of the knowledge of Him in every place* (2 Corinthians 2:14).

2. Do others pick up the scent of Christ in your everyday actions? Who do you know that exemplifies the giving up of self and sacrifice for others, like Jesus did for us? *And walk in love, just as Christ also loved you and gave Himself up for us, an offering and a sacrifice to God as a fragrant aroma* (Ephesians 5:2).

CHAPTER SEVENTEEN

I'm Only Going in Blue

B asically, I'm a pretty big wimp. Letting fear have its way instead of facing it head on is one of my weaknesses. I'm that one who wouldn't consider taking chances with anything the least bit scary. I know. I know. I've missed out on many challenging opportunities which could've possibly been fun. I've heard it for years.

Our closest group of friends began planning a ski trip to Colorado, an experience way out of my comfort zone. The wives chattered excitedly between each other, all except me.

"I have to get new boots."

"I need new goggles."

"I've got to go shopping for a new ski jacket."

I don't think anyone noticed my uncommon quietness in the throes of their exhilaration. I can't blame them, had I not felt fearful, I would have joined right in. But instead of excitement, my anticipation oozed with misery and mental suffering.

For a while I tried to cling to denial, telling myself I wasn't scared, but instead, needed to exercise cautious optimism. Someone in the group needed to keep their feet planted on the ground while everyone else swooshed around. While my friends focused on apparel, I made a checklist of apparent dangers. Preparing for the worst was the best defense weapon in my coping arsenal at the time. But as the date grew closer, I hid my struggle—the fact that I would prefer to say, "Uh, no thanks. Skiing is not for me."

My inner wrestling was magnified by my honey's gung-ho attitude toward the trip. Sometimes you find yourself sliding along, just hoping for the best. I spent many weeks putting the entire scenario before the Lord in prayer. I asked for wisdom, confidence, and occasionally, a good excuse to get me out of this predicament in one piece.

I did have one secret safety net, something I held onto in the back of my mind. The fact was we didn't own any ski clothing or equipment. I just knew this was going to be the deal-breaker resulting in my rescue.

But God . . .

Maybe you've heard people quote these two words, but did you know they can be found in many places in the Bible? If you want to do a fascinating study, search the term "But God" in your favorite Bible app. Then pay close attention to the context and circumstances surrounding those two words. It's a great faith-builder.

When it came to my ski trip, I had hoped God would agree with me, believing we shouldn't participate. I thought instead that He would prefer we stay safe at home and pray for the safety of the others.

But God . . .

My first safety net, the one that said we didn't have enough money in our savings account to warrant the ticket purchase, fell through quickly. My husband, not one to splurge foolishly when it came to financial matters, and someone who always prayed and thought through his decisions, shocked me. Somehow, Mackey felt we could swing the trip. This tore my first safety net to shreds.

But God . . .

My second safety net crumbled into pieces when friends offered to loan Mackey and me some ski clothes, masks, and gloves. Really? This was a rare time when I did not appreciate their generosity.

But God . . .

My third net was torn into bits when a young couple from church offered to stay in our home while we were gone and babysit our two young boys. Who does that?

But God . . .

The net-shredding continued as my fourth and final webbing was breached. Friends offered to let us stay at their parents' home in Memphis, the location of our airplane terminal, free of charge. This kind act enabled us to save extra money by catching the early-bird flight.

But God . . .

Through every disappointing provision, I remained adamant, but fearful, and still prayed that God would put His stops to everything. Strangely enough though, I thought I heard Him whisper that I was not only going, but that I was going in blue.

Blue? I mentally questioned.

Yes, blue.

During the final week of planning, our generous friends dropped off an overly large bag of ski gear at our front door. As I rummaged through its contents, I searched straight through to the bottom of the bag but found no blue attire. *Aha!* I thought. *Confirmation.* However, I was simply running ahead of the Lord's timing.

But God . . .

I believe myself to be a woman of faith, and I certainly believe in the power of prayer and God's answering voice. So where was the blue that I most distinctively heard God speak about in my heart?

Rifling through the bag again, only more slowly this time, I found yellow and red skiwear, but not a tinge of blue. Doubts and hope flooded my heart simultaneously. Was something wrong with my spiritual hearing? Was God going to allow us to remain safely at home with our children? I continued to pray about both.

The day finally arrived, and I had received neither rescue from my attendance on the trip, nor a blue outfit. Mac, I, and our six closest friends, traveled north to spend the night at the lovely home of our other friends from Memphis. After a wonderful meal, we retired to a soft bed, where I finally threw all of my dreams for a surprise safety net to the wind.

But God . . .

The next morning, with my stomach in knots and everything planned out, we headed to the airport in Memphis. Of course, I was still very unsure of this whole dilemma. And though my faith was shaken just a tad, I continued to look to God for help. He'd never let me down before.

Now I had to act as though I was "oh so excited" to go. Couldn't my good friends see through my facade? Well, if they did, they never mentioned it to me. Living behind a mask of fear is most exhausting.

As we walked toward our terminal gate, I looked through the large window to check the size and safety of our plane. A woman of faith should not be the least bit surprised when God delivers on His promises, but I was stunned at what I saw.

It was blue. That's right, the plane was blue. The aircraft sent to carry us from Memphis to Denver was as blue as blue can be. To this day, I don't think I've even seen another blue plane since that one in 1982. True to His word, God was sending me on this ski trip just as He stated. I was going in blue. And I'd assumed He meant my outfit.

At least I was leaving on a jet plane, knowing God was traveling ahead of me. However, even though He'd seen fit to summon a blue plane to prove yet again how trustworthy He is, I still needed help to cast off the rest of my fears.

The thought of riding the ski lift sent shivers up my spine, and not the good kind. This presented my next opportunity to cast off fear, another chance to trust God in all things.

Feeling the earth whoosh out from under my feet tickled my stomach and caused my nerves to churn. But in spite of my anxiety, I spoke faith. Under my breath, yet still loud enough for others to hear, I said, "Be gone, fear." Then I forced my eyes to open, and when I did, my soul could hardly absorb the full scope of breathtaking beauty.

Grand evergreens and tall Aspens graced the mountain face on both sides around us. Massive boulders blended with ancient, volcanic rock, scattered like a child's marbles across deep valleys and high crevices. A lake in the distance reflected the sapphire sky, cotton ball clouds, and sparkling sun of a perfect, winter's day. And fluffy, pristine snow topped everything, adding an air of purity to every gorgeous part of creation my eyes could take in.

In that moment, I realized my ridiculous fear actually enhanced the joy I felt. This glorious view made me appreciate every ounce of angst. The effort to exercise faith and overcome my worries made this experience even more worthwhile. What a gift to be absolutely overwhelmed by God's creativity. I soaked up crazy peace as I rode the lift with dangling legs. I spent the rest of the ride giving God glory for the great things He had done. But I still hadn't faced the top of the mountain.

Reaching the pinnacle temporarily stole my sense of calm. I realized I actually, willingly, had to slide down a slippery snow and ice-covered mountain on two extremely skinny pieces of plastic. Fear attacked me again, but this time I was ready. Sometimes, you have to cast that fear off, over and over again, refusing to let it reside on your shoulders.

I looked down the side of the steep slope, stiffened my spine, took a full breath, and said, "My trust is in the Lord. Be gone, fear!" Then I pushed off.

By the time I got to the bottom, with some degree of success, and injury free, I felt breathless and giddy. Now I wanted to go up again.

Today fear no longer has its grip on me. I know to trust God's voice and to wait patiently on His timing. I can boldly say, "I am an overcomer, but only with You in my life!" This gives me crazy, consistent peace.

The Lord is always faithful, even when some of His children take a little longer than others to release their anxiety and put their confidence wholly in Him. That would be me, for sure. Thankfully, He cares for us even more than He does the birds He so lovingly watches over.

Opening Our Eyes

1. Do you recall a time when God surprised you with His provision? What's the most interesting way God has kept His word to you? *Trust in the Lord with all your heart And do not lean on your own understanding. In all your ways acknowledge Him, And He will make your paths straight* (Proverbs 3:5–6).

2. Have you ever wrestled anxiety over a situation, even though you prayed and tried hard to trust God? Do you listen for God's voice as well as talk to Him? *Having cast all your anxiety on Him, because He cares about you* (1 Peter 5:7).

CHAPTER EIGHTEEN

Glass Deception

It was an exceptionally beautiful day, and the leaves of the trees displayed their delight by frolicking in a slight breeze that whisked by. But as the morning sun began its rise westward, for a brief moment in time it seemed to stop directly overhead. This allowed a few morning shadows to hold the positions they'd cast on my porch.

I was most grateful I had remembered to fill my six bird feeding stations before the last bit of coolness escaped, lost until evening. I had emptied my large bag of mixed seeds, almost to overflowing capacity. But soon, many varieties and multi-sized flocks would arrive, once word of full feeders spread throughout the "bird-dom" community.

News of my full feeders apparently made the rounds quickly. By appearance, all two-winged creatures in the region, even visitors merely passing through, seemed to have received word that a feast was being served up. This announcement drew great crowds, and they began arriving in families and groups of families. I have never understood how the chain of reports, such as filled bird feeders, filters down. But it must be passed by "word-of-beak," for it is quite the sight to behold as fowl of all types position themselves on perches and porches. Each has their preferred flavor.

When the cardinal families visit, they feast on their favorite, sunflower seeds. The brilliantly colored males are always the first to attend the luncheon, then they are shortly followed by the females. "Teen-birds" join the adults, and they all fight for their places at the "perch-table."

This particular morning, I sat at my kitchen table enjoying the warmth of the sun and the entertainment provided by the birds' antics. Suddenly, I was startled by a loud thump on my glass door. *Oh no,* I said to myself. *I do hope that isn't what I think it is.* I arose from my chair, allowing the voice in my head to trail, then be replaced by sorrow and compassion.

After I stepped outside, I found exactly what I suspected. There on my rug, lay a small, greatly stunned, female cardinal. She breathed deeply, struggling to stay alive. Not wanting to work her up further, I kept my distance and watched.

After several minutes, the cardinal flitted around and hopped in a circle, trying to regain her composure. I could tell she'd injured her wing. It obviously took the brunt when she slammed into my house. Apparently, though not exactly sparkling clean, my glass door was sufficiently clear enough to deceive and cause harm to this little one. She probably thought herself safe flying about. She must have misjudged her flight pattern and was therefore stopped cold in her tracks.

I waited for an hour or so before checking on the little cardinal again, hoping she had regained strength and flew away to her family and friends. But no, that wasn't the case. She still sat in the same spot. Then she stretched back to look at me, over her shoulder. I'd never seen a bird behave that way before.

As the cardinal made eye contact with me, I wanted to weep out of pity, but instead, I prayed for her. I knew only her maker, the Lord God of All, knew the plan for her little life. (How long do cardinals live anyway? Google says three to fifteen years.)

I walked away again, but just long enough to quench my thirst. Upon returning, I was surprised to see another bird walking around my patio. I wondered, *Is she checking on her friend or is the disabled cardinal her sibling?* Regardless, what could the healthy bird do for the injured one? Only God knew. I was left to use my imagination.

Maybe the healthy bird was sent out to assess the injured cardinal's situation and arrange help from the family for a rescue later on. Maybe I could help.

Some would say the cardinal was only a bird, but I sensed I should do what I could to assist her. I wanted to know she would be okay.

When I next returned to the scene of the accident, I arrived prayed up. And I decided to do all I knew for the cardinal. One certainty I had was knowing I didn't want my dog to get involved in the situation. I decided I should relocate the cardinal. So I placed a bag over my hand and lifted the fragile contents ever so gently. I then placed her in the shade of a nearby bush, hoping her possible rescue squad could still find her and lend a talon. Later that afternoon, when I checked under the bush, the cardinal was gone. I'm not sure what happened to that little bird, but I do know that, ultimately, her Heavenly Father saw His best plan through for her.

That evening, as I pondered the young bird's fall, I was reminded that I have experienced spiritual disasters equal to the injured cardinal's physical predicament. Any time I have diverted my eyes from my contented nest in life, and longingly looked to the windows of my neighbors' lives, I've aimed directly at the shiny window of comparison. This mostly resulted in subsequent splats.

Too many times I've willingly traded in my joyful nest and crazy peace for the mirage of a seemingly happier place. I've learned that not all full feeders provide healthy endings. Deceptions, like glass doors, can seduce you and draw you away from the blessings and gifts all around you. Beware, discontentment can slam us before we even know what direction the hit came from. Covetousness causes my contented heart to yearn for something beyond what I already have, but the inevitable resulting thud leaves me in a compromising position. When I'm lying on the ground as it were, looking upward, I'm exactly where I need to be—positioned to be set upright again.

Little did my winged friend know, but her splat and fall brought a spiritual truth to mind. No matter what foolish decisions we've made, or what shiny objects have captured our attention and pulled us away from God, He will not leave us laying on the ground. He will tenderly pick us up, tend to our wounds, and set us on course again. Sometimes He will even send someone else to come to our aid. But He never takes His watchful eye off us.

If even the sparrow cannot fall to the ground without His notice, God is monitoring us even more closely. He does not watch so He can catch us doing something wrong, or wait hoping to lash out in punishment. God is ever diligent to protect and save.

Even and especially when we find ourselves in a compromising spiritual position where we lie face up, if we will call out to our Father, we will find Him waiting to come to our faithful rescue. This is what He desires most.

God alone can refresh our joy and restore our crazy peace. A little bird taught me that I should remain ever on guard against deceptions which will seduce me with their glaring shine. And it's not the only time God used a feathered friend. Many challenges, problems, and fears ultimately transform into opportunities for thanking God, some small, and some are absolutely ginormous.

Opening Our Eyes

1. When has God restored you after a fall? To what lengths do you think God will go to in order to save you? *Are two sparrows not sold for an assarion? And yet not one of them will fall to the ground apart from your Father* (Matthew 10:29).

2. Do you pay attention to the devotion your Heavenly Father shows the birds of the air, realizing He cares even more for you? Do you feel important to God? *Look at the birds of the sky, that they do not sow, nor reap, nor gather crops into barns, and yet your heavenly Father feeds them. Are you not much more important than they?* (Matthew 6:26).

CHAPTER NINETEEN

Wrangling the Ginormous

We didn't know we needed them until the cutting was done. We had to call on our new neighbors (I'd just met the wife the day before), to come to our rescue with their truck. What would you do if the perfect Christmas tree you just felled exceeded the size limitations of your vehicle? Before I tell you more about the tree story though, let me first explain how we met our rescuers.

It was the kind of gray, cool day Georgia attributes to the onset of winter. After hours of unloading in an ongoing misty rain, the moving truck finally drove away. Just as the movers were completely out of sight, I stepped into the yard to greet the young family who had just arrived in our neighborhood.

"Hi, I'm Jill," the wife said cheerily. "This is my husband, Chuck, and our three-year-old daughter, Kimberly."

"It's nice to meet you," I said. "We live next door. Welcome to the neighborhood."

I bent down to their little girl's height. "Hi, Kimberly, I'm Miss Linda, and this is my daughter, Micah." I pulled my three-year-old daughter from her glued-to-my-side position and placed her in front of me.

Kimberly smiled shyly, and eked out a weak, "Hi," while clutching the edge of her mama's pleated yellow skirt.

"Look, girls, you have matching purple raincoats." I pointed to the similar colors in their outerwear.

They were two peas in a pod. It was as if they were always meant to be "best-est friends," as they would soon call themselves. God had again answered a prayer when Mackey and I asked Him to provide friends for our kids.

Chuck and Mac quickly found they shared interests too. Their fascination with golf was the center of many conversations.

Starting on the day we met, Jill and I hit it off. I invited her to "come on over for a cup of coffee" and she gladly complied.

"A short break would be nice after the stress of directing box placements all day," she said. "How long have you lived here?"

"We've been here right at five years," I said. "Mackey's work means periodic transfers for our family."

"We came over from Florida when Chuck got transferred," Jill said. "Isn't God good? Here we are, total strangers who lived states apart, but with so much in common, who God put together at the same place and time. I just love when He organizes my life for me."

"I couldn't agree more."

Jill and I, already bonded as friends, hugged tightly. Just before she walked out the door, Jill turned back. "Oh, do you know of any Christmas tree farms nearby? We need to get ours sometime this week."

I laughed. "There we go, right on the same page again. We like to get our tree early, too, and always go to Taylor's Tree Farm. Let me grab their info for you."

I laughed at multiple similarities I had already discovered between us and Chuck and Jill. God's hand certainly seemed to be behind orchestrating our introductions. Little did we know, we'd soon see more evidence of God's coordinating plans.

The crispness of late fall air made things even better the next day. Mac and I headed to the tree farm with gloves, a hacksaw, some rope, and three extremely excited kids in tow. The sky seemed even bluer than normal, which made for a perfect backdrop as we leaned our heads back to see the tippy-top rows in an elegant forest of cultivated evergreens.

The kids ran ahead, and the five of us searched high and low for that perfect tree. We struggled to make our selection, because the choices were numerous.

I jogged behind the kids until they got distracted by starting an impromptu game of tag. I stopped with them and allowed myself several seconds to breathe in the joy of their laughter. The rare moment of crazy peace in the midst of an everyday errand soothed my soul to its depth. Then I noticed what was right in front of me.

The perfect specimen stood straight and tall. The tree seemed to nearly reach the heavens. "This is the one," I said reverently, not realizing my entire family had gathered around me until I heard them all murmur agreement. Even my engineer husband did not debate my choice.

With an engineer's precision, Mackey started the chopping, giving our five- and nine-year-old boys a token turn, to dispel their begging. This tree, our tree, towered above the many others surrounding it. We were so happy with our choice, and all seemed well, until a thought entered my mind.

I pictured the massive evergreen atop our minivan and realized we were in deep trouble. The tree would hang at least two to three feet each over the front and back, if not longer. I imagined the weight of the ginormous fir popping all four tires simultaneously. We hadn't thought ahead to how we would transport our beloved specimen from the tree farm to our living room. Suddenly, cracking timber warned me that we'd better come up with a fast solution. Mackey's sharp ax finally felled our tree. I began to pray—fervently.

A honking horn announced the arrival of a large truck as it topped the hill. I couldn't believe God answered so quickly. Our new "best-est" friends, Chuck and Jill waved from the cab.

Waving back, I wondered, *Do we dare ask them for help? Will they think we're imposing?*

Chuck and Jill parked and got out. Before I had an opportunity to voice my thoughts, Mackey surprised me by speaking up. "I hate to ask, but I think our eyes were bigger than our van. Is there any chance we could ask a huge favor? Could you possibly haul our tree home for us? We'll gladly pay you for the gas and your time."

"Not a problem at all, neighbor," Chuck said. "And no need to pay us a dime. I'm sure you'll return the favor sometime." He paused momentarily. "Well, maybe not this exact favor." We all laughed.

It took a while for Mackey and Chuck to load our monstrous timber choice next to Chuck and Jill's much smaller version. But once secured, we pulled out ahead of our neighbors. Our over-anxious brood acted out in antsy fashion, the boys cracking jokes about Chuck's funny looking truck with both trees on top.

With our ability to drive at a much faster pace, we pulled in our driveway far ahead of Chuck and Jill. This gave us time to rearrange all of the furniture in our den, so we could make space for our chosen giant.

Impatient, the children repeatedly asked, "What's taking them so long? When are they going to get here?"

When the truck slowly backed into our driveway, the kids hooped and hollered. Mac met Chuck at the truck, and the two men proceeded to unstrap our ginormous Christmas tree. Using a dolly cart on each end, one pushing forward and one pulling backwards, the men wheeled the tree through our doorway. Well, forced is probably a more accurate word. Looking at the monstrosity in our den, it was even more evident that we had practiced very little willpower in the choosing of our evergreen. We were in for more challenges than Mackey or I had anticipated.

In retrospect, I'm shocked that my common-sense husband did not nix my request while we were still at the farm. Maybe it was the fact that we had a cathedral ceiling in our den that caused Mackey to let my ginormous choice slide. But I don't think even he realized we were going to try and cram a White House-sized tree into our regular-house-sized den. Regardless, he was a trooper.

Mackey trimmed the misshaped branches off, but because the tree was so tall, he had to cut another foot off the top, just so our angel could take her rightful place. Otherwise she would've had to bend her head down or lean over to one side to protect her golden halo. And the drama didn't end there.

The tree was so large that the four large bolts in our tree stand would not secure it. Thankfully, my engineering husband came to the rescue. He sent the boys to his tool room, bellowing, "Get the fishing line!"

The tree had to be secured near the top as well as the bottom. So, teetering on a ladder, Mackey wrapped the clear fishing line round and round the tree's sawed-off crown. He then instructed me to take the end of the inconspicuous line, walk it through the kitchen, the dining room, and then back again into the family room. He used the small dividing wall between those three rooms as the anchor for our monster tree. Mackey tugged on the line until it was taut, and then had me walk the end of the line through the same maze of rooms three more times, before he tied it off.

Success!

Finally, the piney giant stood on its own, majestically tall and somewhat straight. Mackey backed up to take a look at his endeavor, then smiled. It was a hard job, but I could feel the sense of satisfaction oozing from my husband's pores. His joy was short-lived, however, when he realized we still had to decorate and string lights, his least favorite Christmas activity. And this year, we were going to need a lot of extras.

Because of my annual hobby of collecting ornaments for each child, there were plenty of baubles and trinkets to mix with an ample amount of candy canes, so our massive tree was adequately trimmed. When the final treasure was hung on the last branch, we all stepped back to take in the wonderous sight.

Our ginormous Christmas tree was the biggest and most breathtaking I'd ever seen, and I suddenly saw it with spiritual eyes. Through the process of reaching this moment, we'd each endured excitement, anticipation, humility, frustration, impatience, momentary worry, and joy. The experience also allowed us to feel God's crazy peace around us.

Yes, the holidays can be hard and stressful, but as we found out that year, the greater the challenge, the sweeter the celebration. Let's face it, none of us have faced any pains even close to what Jesus endured on the cross by giving up His life to pay for our sins.

So if the worst thing we had to go through was wrangling a towering evergreen, we were happy to do it. The attitude we view things through is half the battle, after all, right? Lying in bed that night, I could imagine God saying to Mackey, "Well done, good and faithful servant," for his hard work and patience. There's no greater reward than that. Even when we're questioning where God is calling us to go, our Heavenly Father's desire is to tell us good job.

Opening Our Eyes

---

1. Have you ever met someone and felt as if God had orchestrated your introduction? Do you know what traits we are to demonstrate, based on Christ's commands, to be called His friend? *You are My friends if you do what I command you* (John 15:14).

2. Do you remember a time when you plunged into a project, or bought something, without first calculating and measuring? Has God ever shown you grace when you made a decision without first consulting Him? *For which one of you, when he wants to build a tower, does not first sit down and calculate the cost, to see if he has enough to complete it?* (Luke 14:28).

God's Crazy Peace
of Assurance

CHAPTER TWENTY

Birds, Trains, and Parking Spaces

When God redirects our paths, many times we are surprised at His creativity. But why? After all, He did create the entire universe with nothing more than His breath and a few words. I've learned that seeing God's hand requires us to open our eyes. One situation really drove this truth home for me a few years back.

My husband, Mackey, was facing another job transfer which meant our nineteenth move (yes, that's a literal number) to a new abode, relocating from Atlanta to Mississippi. Each change of address meant stretching my trust in God. However, the Mississippi move pushed me to an even deeper test of faith. It required listening for God's voice, then watching and waiting with belief, before I actually saw the fruition of the promise God had whispered to my mind and spirit.

Our move to Mississippi led us back to apartment dwelling, while our home in Georgia sat unsold for eight months. House hunting felt impossible, but we continued in prayer, holding onto the Ephesians 3:20 assurance that in my paraphrase says, God will "do exceedingly, abundantly beyond all that we ask, think, dream, or hope."

So we asked. We sought. We knocked. We waited in faith with our eyes and ears wide open. And in the process, my husband and I had the opportunity to see God work in a very unique manner. God became our realtor. I distinctively heard Him whisper to my mind, "You'll have birds, trains, and parking spaces." I confess, the oddity of His message made me question.

"Wait, what, Lord?" I said.

I felt His confirmation. "Yes, birds, trains, and parking spaces."

When I shared the experience with a couple of my Georgia friends, they wondered out loud if I was moving to a state park. All I could do was reiterate what I heard God say. I had no explanation for the strange promise. I could only believe His familiar voice and wait on Him.

As Mackey and I toured homes, we found most were more than lovely and would fit our family and budget just fine. However, some didn't allow for street parking, and those with just two allotted parking spaces could not accommodate our family of six when our adult children came for visits.

During those eight months of waiting and faith-testing, I admit I fell for many houses, but then the deal would disintegrate when our Georgia property didn't sell. We were tempted to settle a couple of times but chose to trust instead. We knew we'd recognize the right dwelling when God revealed and confirmed it. The search stretched on and on and on, until finally, the perfect family bought our Georgia home. To close the deal, we temporarily suspended our hunt for a house in Mississippi and headed back to Atlanta for the pack and move.

We breathed a little easier once we got all of our household belongings into storage in the vicinity of Mac's new job. But we also felt time-pressured to find our new home since his company had only provided thirty days of storage for us. After that, we'd have to foot the bill. So I rushed back to Mississippi to continue the home search.

Now starting over, I decided to check out the neighborhoods we had liked, but this time searched for "non-stucco" options. Mac's company had told us they would not purchase our house if it had stucco on it if we were transferred again. There are often issues with rot beneath a stucco veneer. Our realtor had included several stucco options in the *For Sale* flyers she gave us to look through, so weeding them out reduced the stack. I plunged into the down-sized pile, knowing God was ultimately in control. I trusted He already knew where our new home was located. Yet, the testing of my faith continued on. Little did I know that He was about to amaze us with His choice.

Many of the houses the realtor showed us had bird feeders out back, and this intrigued me, as I pondered God's promise of birds, trains, and parking spaces. But each time we visited one of these homes, we found they just didn't make the cut. Onward we pressed.

While continuing my review of our prospects via drive-by visits, I decided to eliminate a particular one-street neighborhood. As I left, I drove toward the cul-de-sac and saw a *For Sale by Owner* sign in the yard of a beautiful brick house with a wide, spacious driveway. I pulled over and jotted down the phone number.

I called immediately and asked for an appointment.

"We're scheduled to show it to someone else on Saturday," the homeowner said.

"Oh, I understand." Disappointment dripped from my voice.

"I guess you could come take a look at it on Thursday, if you want."

"We'll be there," I said, daring to let a sliver of hope trickle through my veins.

Thursday arrived, bringing an all-day torrential downpour. It was the kind of rain where an umbrella was futile. When we pulled into the driveway of the brick house, we parked as close to the entrance as possible and ran for the safety of the front door. While standing beneath the small eave over the front porch, we wiped rain off of each other's shoulders. I shivered as Mackey pressed the doorbell. Then we heard a commotion. We both looked up, and there it was.

A bird was caught under the eave of the house, and it squawked while struggling to free itself. Just before the homeowner opened the door to welcome us inside, the bird got loose and flew away. Watching in wonder, I pondered. *Could it be? Is this a sign? Have we found our promised house with birds, trains, and parking spaces?*

The homeowner led us into the open living area and invited us to explore with the sweep of her left arm. As if pulled by an invisible rope, Mackey and I both walked straight to the large picture window at the far end of the room, showcasing a beautiful pond out back. The homeowner asked us to excuse her while she went to the office to print out some specifics regarding the home. It was then, while standing alone, that Mac turned to me.

He said, "I don't need to see it."

I almost screeched, "What's not to like?" But instead, waited for my husband to explain himself.

Before he started talking, I evaluated my shock at his remark. This was the man who had climbed into the attics of other houses we viewed to inspect the bones of the structure and to check the heating and air. How could he disregard this house so quickly? He saw the bird as well as I did. And how could he miss the size of the driveway? I'd told him about God's message to me. I was shocked that Mac wasn't willing to at least give this house a chance.

Interrupting my mental rant, Mackey put his arm around my shoulder and guided me closer toward the window. "I believe this is it. This is our new home." As if on signal, a train whistle sounded ever so faintly in the distance.

Relief flooded my soul. I leaned my head on my husband's shoulder and sighed.

Mackey and I spent the next two hours experiencing God's reassurance, including the fact that the man and his wife selling the house also had a strong faith in Jesus Christ as their Savior. Our initial instincts were right, we were home!

The next day, we returned with our checkbook in hand to pay the earnest money. But when Mac held out the check, the man said, "A handshake will do."

In no time, we were excitedly unpacking boxes and setting up rooms. The dread of relocating didn't affect us like a lot of people, moving was an old habit.

After we settled in, we discovered just how specific God had been in keeping His word about providing birds, trains, and parking spaces. Through the years, we enjoyed watching a large collection of fowl, including white egrets, blue herons, Canadian geese, cow birds, Mallard ducks, and buffleheads. (We had to look that last one up in a bird book.) They were often accompanied by the usual backyard varieties of cardinals, bluebirds, sparrows, blue jays, and robins.

At regular intervals (you could usually set your clocks by the train schedules), we'd hear the whistle blow in the background. Our family found comfort in the distant noise that signaled a train's approach to nearby crossings. If you listened closely, you could even hear their wheels turning on the tracks.

And parking spaces? Well, God not only provided, but He provided to our exact requirements. Prior to closing, we realized our driveway comfortably accommodated four vehicles and the garage could fit two more. We needed six when all of our children gathered with their families, and that's precisely what we received. Again, I found that what God says will always come true.

Faith means praying to God, listening, waiting on Him, but doing so with absolute trust. We must keep our eyes open to see His provision when it comes, and it will come. There is no need for worry—we can have crazy peace in any circumstance—assured God is always faithful and true. And when you're buying or selling a house, it's comforting to know He is also THE best realtor of all. God's fingerprints offer ongoing proof of His unending provision and care.

Opening Our Eyes

1. If we believe everything belongs to God, why do you think we worry or fear? Do you ever consider God's ownership of your everyday possessions, and how He might provide for your smallest needs? *For every animal of the forest is Mine, the cattle on a thousand hills* (Psalm 50:10).

2. Most of us know how to talk to God, but sometimes we are unsure when it comes to hearing Him. Do you know how to listen for and recognize God's voice? *My sheep listen to My voice, and I know them, and they follow Me* (John 10:27).

CHAPTER TWENTY-ONE

Forever Fingerprints
of Fury

T he worst day of the year is the day you have to leave the beach. Agreed? The relaxing sounds of those continually crashing waves, the squawks of happy seagulls, the taste of salty breezes kissing your lips, and the gritty-squishy feel of sand surrounding your toes. Every beachy sense points to sheer rejuvenating delight.

When I'm sitting by the water's edge, I relish four R's: refreshment, relaxation, relief, and restoration, though it never seems long enough. At home, my weary body and brain desperately yearn to trade my sometimes mundane life for a week of chill time. I could live by the salt and sand.

For forty-one years, every June our family filled up multiple condos for a week of fun under the sun. This annual trip provided priceless benefits in building and strengthening our relationships. The congregating routine especially helped, since our family members at last count were scattered across ten states.

During our cherished week, cousins enjoyed cousins, while aunts and uncles truly got to know their nieces and nephews. At the beach, Grandma and Grandpa finally had time and permission to spoil their twenty-three grandchildren. A lot of intentionality went into making it all work.

The smartest thing we ever did was meal planning. When you have the food covered, most everything else falls into place. At the very least, you don't have to deal with a hungry mob. We decided each family would take responsibility for cooking dinner one day of our week and feed the entire crew. When your turn to prepare rolled around, it meant a lot of work, but that effort paid off for the rest of our vacation. The reward from cooking much of one day meant you could linger on the beach or poolside, then be served hors d'oeuvres and summoned for dinner, without lifting a finger for the rest of the week. It felt amazing to simply relax most of the trip. For years, we followed that successful formula and a few others. However, not everything went as I hoped.

Annually, upon our arrival at the condo, I automatically underwent the same strategic transformation. I'm a bit embarrassed to admit that I unofficially, but mentally, handed my family over to some of our other loved ones for the week. I desperately attempted to melt into oblivion, hoping to be unneeded, maybe even unseen, for just this one week a year. If you're a wife and mom, maybe you understand my secret desire. Sometimes, you get tired of hearing your own name.

Since my husband was one of nine children, there were plenty of relatives to go around. Each year followed a similar pattern. I mentally released my four kids into the loving hands of our extended family and watched them morph into nieces, nephews, cousins, and grandchildren. In like manner, my husband stepped into the shoes of a brother, brother-in-law, uncle, and son to mingle with those awaiting his undistracted attention. Mackey was always known as the fun uncle.

Since I am a die-hardened list-maker, forever attempting to get my ducks in a row, I maintained an annual packing list—printed, of course. The essential items atop my list were the menus, recipes, and shopping lists for my turn at preparing meals for our week. Even one night of culinary prowess for thirty to forty hungry souls required serious organization. My detailed grocery list looked more like a pamphlet than a piece of paper—without the other beach essentials.

Besides bathing suits, one of the most important and challenging choices you'll make for a trip to the seaside is deciding on your suntan lotion. These days, there are a myriad of brands and SPF numbers, ranging from fifteen to seventy-five, so settling on one can feel challenging. One thing I learned the hard way, is to read the application directions and warnings for various lotions. I confess I hadn't previously done that and found out some outcomes do not go unnoticed if misapplied.

On one eventful beach excursion, immediately following lunch, my honey and I headed out for some sun, surf, and tan time. He went for the surf, and I went for the tan. We both enjoyed the sun. As soon as we settled our chairs, bags, and towels, we took turns lathering each other's backs. That's what good spouses do, right?

How many of us know that living in close quarters for a full week can sometimes produce tension? On this particular morning, when either something was said or not said to my liking, I can't recall which, I felt exceptionally frustrated with Mac. Regardless of its origin, the consequence of this small something is now forever etched in my memory.

After Mackey applied lotion to my back, I took the tube and quickly squirted a gigantic glob on his back and shoulders. With gritted teeth, I angrily slid just my fingertips through the lotion, dragging part of it from his shoulders to his waistline. (I did not use my fingernails, but in all sincerity, the thought did cross my mind.) I pulled the white goop downward as fast as possible and left my distinct embedded fingerprints for all to see. I didn't bother spreading it out to finish the job smoothly.

A little while later, when we packed up for the day, evidence of my mad reaction was imprinted on my husband's back. Still feeling miffed and justified due to the now forgotten infraction, I kept my mouth clamped shut. *Let him find out on his own*, I thought.

Not one to hold grudges, it didn't take long for me to forgive Mackey and whatever catalyst launched our fight. I quickly forgot about it. But I also buried the memory of my outburst on the beach.

I guess busyness and lack of focus caused me to overlook my husband's back, at least until I couldn't avoid it. Two summers came and went without me giving our incident another thought. Then again at our favorite rest haven, Mac and I headed to the beach. I prepared to slather his back with protection again, only this time with a much better mindset. But what I saw when my husband removed his shirt made me pause.

Though faint, the etched markings of my "forever fingerprints of fury" from two summers before were still visible. I would've thought that twenty-four months would provide ample time for skin cells to slough off the proof of my secret crime. But there was no mistaking the corroborating outline spurred by my angry spirit, so long ago. I remembered I'd never told Mackey. He was oblivious to what I had done.

"Honey, I have something to tell you," I said sheepishly. You can imagine how the rest of our conversation played out.

In hindsight, I can see how God did not waste this unique opportunity to humble me. I apologized repeatedly, stumbling over my words to anxiously tell Mackey how sorry I was. Better late than never, right?

Being the loving husband he was, Mackey graciously agreed to forgive me and did so rather quickly. After all, those body-surfing waves were calling out his name—he had more fun things to focus on. God's crazy peace was clearly at the core of Mac's response. Besides, I think he saw more humor in the situation than I did. I felt too guilty to share in his good-natured chuckling.

Now that Mackey is no longer with me, I would give whatever I had to go back now and have a re-do. The frustration I felt at the time of my fingerprint fiasco likely came from something that didn't matter much. With a better understanding about how small many concerns really are in comparison to the shortness of our lives together, I would have taken the time to show him my love rather than my fury. It's best to work things out before the sun goes down, so you can live a life without wishes for do-overs.

Though I know Mackey and I will see each other in eternity someday, and God carries me through life on the wings of His crazy peace, I still carry a few regrets. For those instances, I think: *If only I had another chance. If only I had reacted differently. If only I had listened to the Holy Spirit's voice instead of my own angry self-talk. If only!*

Opening Our Eyes

1. When have you lost your cool and regretted your reaction? Can you remember a time you spontaneously did something out of spite, only to have it create lasting consequences? *For I know my wrongdoings, and my sin is constantly before me* (Psalm 51:3).

2. Can you recall a time when you lost sleep because of anger? How do you ensure conflicts are resolved before bedtime? *Be angry, and yet do not sin; do not let the sun go down on your anger* (Ephesians 4:26).

CHAPTER TWENTY-TWO

His Voice, Your Story

Voice. It's something most all people have. Our mammas probably said, "Lower your voice, use your inside voice," or "keep your voice down." Yet, your drama teacher or vocal coach would say, "Project your voice for all to hear." That voice, whether used to yell or to whisper, lets others know you have something worthy, important, or even secretive to say.

We have each been gifted with an inner voice—one that represents you and me more fully. Whether we are timid and shy, or the loudest one in the room who grabs the attention of all, the real you shines via your voice.

I read a quote once that said, *Your story is your truth.*

For years, I've said, "We all have a book inside of us. It's called our voice. It's what we think, feel, and experience. Our stories can connect us with others."

We live our whole lives hearing that no two people are created alike. And it's true. Even if you and I witnessed the same event, we could honestly describe it from totally different viewpoints. Our takeaways can differ just as our fingerprints do. And our perception based on personal temperament, history, and current environment will impact how we address any topic.

Before we go any further, let's be clear. There is no wrong voice—all are pertinent and deserve to be heard. The individuality of each of our voices reveal the truth of who we are, but it is often buried deep inside. Not everyone feels free to use their voice.

Whether by choice or conditioning, many people squash their true thoughts down into the hidden recesses of their minds. This usually happens as a result of past or present shaming, being made to believe they're not worthy or good enough to be heard.

However, once they learn to overcome these outside influences which made them feel intimidated, rejected, or inferior, peeling back layers of discouragement becomes possible. Only then can they step out of the shadows and walk fully in the light of their truth. This allows the world to hear, enjoy, and listen to their voice.

So what are you withholding? There is always a need for people to hear positive and motivating messages. Who knows the encouragement you might bring to others who have shared similar experiences as you? How can you become a tool for good in someone else's life? There's potential purpose waiting in your past.

I encourage you, even urge you, to pull out a pen and some paper and let her rip. Get your phone or computer and begin typing. Regardless of the tools or methods you use, engage your thoughts and transfer them into written form. Use your voice and put it in black and white, whether you ever intend to show it to another soul or not. But if you do choose to share, I for one want to read it.

But if your voice has long been shrouded by fear and discouragement or feels too tender to risk getting trampled on, let me assure you, I understand. If your voice is loud and strong, but suppressed for far too long, I know what it's like to wonder, *where do I start?*

I've had to bring my own voice to these pages, but only after receiving the encouragement of others, and I want to pass it on to you. I know what it's like to be wrapped in layers of insecurity. I used to struggle inwardly, thinking, *I don't know how to turn my thoughts into a book.* For me, it all started with a single goal that I spoke out loud for no one but myself to hear. I told the ceiling, "I will get these stories off my computer in 2020."

For years, among family, friends, and those my writings were passed on to, I used my voice to tell my stories—some silly and some serious. You've already read some of them as I've opened up my heart in this book. But my deepest desire is for you to see God in the experiences I share. I want you to grasp a tiny part of His love for you. I want you to see His goodness and character in how He helps us in our everyday events. I want you to know God's yearning for an intimate relationship with you. Through true stories from my own life, I want you to see how God is willing to work in yours.

Since God is the Creator of us all and we are made in His image and yet unique, we each have a voice with the ability to tell of His uniqueness within us. It's God's message, but we put it into human words. Since He can never be fully described, we each have a job to do—to share our voice about Him and His workings in our lives. This allows us to add to His story for others to learn from and enjoy.

My pen cannot possibly reveal the depths of God's massiveness, or how Immanuel, God with us, shows up every day on our behalf. He is the One who bows down to hear the desires of our hearts and lavishly whispers His great love for those willing to listen. It's up to us to shout that good news to the world. From the beginning of time, Immanuel's crazy peace was and is with us.

In 1 Kings 19:11–13, Elijah sought to listen to the Lord. Paraphrased, it says God told him to stand on the mountain, and then the Lord passed by. There was a great and strong wind which crumbled the mountain into rocks, but the Lord was not in the wind. After the wind, there was an earthquake, but the Lord was not in the earthquake. After the earthquake, there was a fire, but the Lord was not in the fire. After the fire, there came a sound of a gentle blowing. Could this be the Lord?

God speaks through His Holy Spirit, who dwells inside of us, once we believe. This Helper, this Comforter, this One who fills us with the fruit of God's Spirit, is the same One who leads, guides, teaches, directs, and encourages us to use our voices. He is the One who reminds us of all the amazing things God is doing in our lives.

So as you consider the small part you play in God's big story, be ready to boldly transcribe it for the audience given to you. Stop and listen on a regular basis. Do you hear His still, small voice? Pay close attention, you never know when He will want you to bear witness to a miracle.

Opening Our Eyes

---

1. How do you think God wants you to use your voice for a greater good? What message do you feel lead to share? *They raise their voices, they shout for joy; They cry out from the west concerning the majesty of the Lord* (Isaiah 24:14).

2. Have you dared to bravely speak your dreams and desires to the Lord? Do you believe God listens to you? Why or why not? *My voice rises to God, and I will cry aloud; My voice rises to God, and He will listen to me* (Psalm 77:1).

CHAPTER TWENTY-THREE

Nine-Year-Old Miracle

There are times when we are called to minister to others. But if we aren't careful, ministry can become so routine, that we can serve almost automatically and robotically, until God pulls out all of His stops.

I've learned we cannot out-give God because we always receive more from Him than we pour into others. He stretches our faith in the process of the giving, sometimes in mustard seed increments, and at other times, through blessings almost too much for us to handle.

Frequently, He not only allows us to see His hand at work in people's lives, but He actually grows us in the situation. I picture Him looking at our faith, then cracking open the windows of heaven to pour an exceedingly abundant amount of increase to it. The results can appear unimaginable!

Such was the case one night when I witnessed a touch of His miraculous power. I was praying, but honestly wasn't expecting Him to act as powerfully as He did.

Our church created a Care Center, welcoming the physically and spiritually hungry people in our area to come for help and hope. Prior to opening the doors for community members to enter, we gathered and prayed for all of those who graced our property.

Each Monday night, the foyer filled to overflow. Humble people, willing to bring their needs to God, were met by Christians willing to lend their hands, hearts, and feet to meet them. Early on, I met Jose, a Hispanic pastor, and I could tell we were kindred spirits from the start.

Pastor Jose and I were both assigned as spiritual counselors. We prayed with the broken hearted, the broken in spirit, and those with physically broken bodies as well. Every Monday night blessed me, but one in particular stood out as a real monumental moment in my life.

Jose was ministering to a Hispanic mother who was wailing with her whole being. Her nine-year-old son was diagnosed with a tumor which stunted his growth. She was told that he would never grow any taller than he was at that time. But to make the situation worse, he was teased at school. Even his teacher did not show the boy any compassion. The woman's sadness felt contagious.

This hurting woman reached out to us in desperation. We wanted to help her but felt totally inadequate. All we were qualified to do was pray, unsure of how God would move.

Jose had already spent some time listening to the young mom and tried to comfort her. He soon asked me to join them in prayer for her little son. Since he was a pastor, I was quite surprised that he asked me to lead the call for God's intervention. I felt insufficient for the task.

I held the woman's hands and smiled at her, unable to speak even the most basic Spanish dialect. I wasn't sure what to pray, but that's not a problem for the Holy Spirit. He "makes intercession for us with groanings too great for us to understand."

Jose and I lifted the woman and her son up to our Father. As I prayed, Jose translated our words from English to Spanish. Only God understands all the languages that humans speak.

When the prayer ended, we hugged the mom and gave her the boxes of food she needed for her family. I felt a bit deflated, wondering if my prayer went anywhere at all. But obviously God had other plans for this woman.

It was a couple of months later before I saw the woman again at the care center. I missed her arrival, but after Jose greeted her, he spent a few minutes searching the hallway until he tracked me down. He called me aside and asked if I remembered the lady and praying for her son's need.

"Of course," I said. No one else had ever asked me to pray about a tumor, so there was no way I'd have forgotten. I noted the big smile on Jose's beaming face.

Jose pointed down the hall and stumbled over his words as he began to tug at my arm, dragging me with him. "You've, you've got to see this. You won't believe it. Just won't. Wait. You'll see it for yourself. Thank you, God!"

What is he talking about? I was too stunned at Jose's behavior to question him out loud. I'd never seen him behave this way before.

We approached a young woman with dark hair wearing a floral dress and black flats. She stood next to a boy wearing khakis and a brightly colored T-shirt, his black hair was slicked into place behind his ears. Jose stopped. Mother and son both had their backs to us, so they didn't notice our arrival, and I did not recognize them. Until they turned around.

Jose tapped the woman on the shoulder, and she turned, her son mimicking his mother's motion. At first, her mocha-colored eyes were pointed toward the floor, as if she needed to take an inferior posture to whomever had wanted her attention. But when she lifted her gaze and recognized Jose, she grinned. When she caught sight of me, however, a slight squeal of delight escaped her throat.

She started babbling in Spanish, and though I had no idea what she was saying, the excitement in her voice told me she was happy to see me. Her countenance had lightened so much from the terrified young mom I'd met previously. Her son, the healthy-looking boy standing shyly next to her with his hands in his pockets, looked completely different from what I remembered. I'd prayed for him because of his brain tumor, but now he appeared transformed.

I smiled at the woman and nodded, hoping to acknowledge her, even if I could not communicate with words. Then she pushed the boy toward me.

He shuffled his feet nervously, eyes downcast.

His mama encouraged him. I understood her directive, though it wasn't in my native tongue. "Della las gracias a ella." I knew she meant, "Tell her thank you."

He obediently said the words.

Then Jose told me the good news, the happy secret that explained their joy. I was about to have my faith strengthened in an amazing way.

"The boy," Jose said, "his name is Rene. His mother told me that the week after we prayed, Rene had another doctor's appointment. This doctor said he had never seen anything like it, for he could not find the tumor. It's a miracle. He is healed. The tumor is gone!"

Now, that kind of news will knock you off your feet, and my knees literally buckled. I had to lean back against the wall and catch my breath to absorb what I had just heard. In a rare moment for me, I had no words. I didn't know what to say, so I stood in silence, relishing the news and giving joyous praise to our God, the Great Healer.

When I finally gathered my composure, I asked permission to take their photo. To this day, I keep the smiling image of a young mother and her son, Rene, in my Bible. The photo symbolizes God's power, reminding me that truly, nothing is impossible with Him. It adds to my crazy peace when I face a difficult situation.

I'll never forget that Monday night when amidst the crowd coming for free groceries and prayer, Jose and I were witnesses to Almighty God in action. He reached down and touched a young boy with His healing hand and strengthened our faith as a result.

Having no understanding of a language doesn't disqualify you from sharing the good news of Christ. God will translate as needed. Feeling insufficient and insecure does not mean you are incapable. God is responsible for the miracle—we are responsible for demonstrating trust in spite of our fears. Always expect God to show up.

Nothing is too difficult for the Lord! We never know when or who He will touch through us, but we are called to be obedient and pray, believing in His power. Even when our faith is weak, his faithfulness remains strong. But we should remember that as followers of Jesus Christ, we have authority over all things when we pray in faith, in Jesus' name. God will answer according to His will.

Every time I open my Bible, I see that photo of Rene and his mom. I think, *Lord, use me again and again for Your glory. Here am I, send me.* We are made to make a difference, and there is no better way to point people to God, the name above all names, than through the power of prayer. The Lord also has the power to reveal.

Opening Our Eyes

1. How has God shown up in a mighty way during a time of weakness for you? What does it mean to you knowing that you don't have to be strong all of the time, and can allow God to carry some of your burdens? *And He has said to me, "My grace is sufficient for you, for power is perfected in weakness." Most gladly, therefore, I will rather boast about my weaknesses, so that the power of Christ may dwell in me* (2 Corinthians 12:9).

2. When have you personally witnessed a prayer miracle? What is the most impossible situation you have seen God make possible? *Oh, Lord God! Behold, You yourself have made the heavens and the earth by Your great power and by Your outstretched arm! Nothing is too difficult for You* (Jeremiah 32:17).

CHAPTER TWENTY-FOUR

Baby Name Reveal

N omenclature? This odd sounding label either represents the process of choosing a name, or the term of applying one to something or someone. No matter your name, each name matters. You're the only one who can be you. God had a particular plan when He created you, and you're the sole person who can bring Him glory in precisely the way He planned.

The Word of God, a.k.a. Bible, is filled with nuggets of truth for us to learn from. In it, He teaches us about Himself and how to live life fully, in a way that satisfies us and glorifies Him. Each name in the Bible represents a particular individual, handmade by God alone. Even in the naming of these people, there is an essential lesson.

Long ago, names bore a message to the bearer, and the people they came in contact with. A parent either labeled a child with encouragement or placed a heavy burden on him/her. Those with a negative name often spent their lifetimes struggling to prove their worthiness—even to themselves.

In the book of Genesis, describing the beginning of all creation, we learn of the Most Holy God. He is also known by Jehovah, the Latin term for His Hebrew proper name, as the God of Israel.[1] He was and is so holy that His name was not ever written down. Instead, it was represented by a mere sound—something like "ah."

As a sign of His covenant with Abram, the Most Holy God exchanged names with him, a mere mortal. God imparted a portion of His holy and unspeakable name to Abram as proof of His part of their intimate relationship. The Lord changed Abram to Abraham and his wife Sarai became Sarah. There's an even more striking fact many miss—God took on Abraham's name as part of His own. The Lord became known as "the God of Abraham." What an outward sign of His great love. I feel like I understand the depth of emotion God felt toward Abraham, His chosen child.

As vetaran parents, my husband and I were overwhelmed with joy when we learned we were expecting our fourth child. We knew that names held great importance. We respected the special influence we would have over this

1 https://en.wikipedia.org/wiki/Jehovah

little one, from designating the name that would follow them throughout their lives, to daily parenting. Mackey and I wielded the power to mark this child for life.

We understood the Lord fully knows each child before a parent ever gets to hold them in their arms. We knew God forms each child in their mother's womb. So, with that knowledge in mind, we began making our lists of both male and female names. We wanted a special nomenclature for this little bundle snuggled inside of me.

But then the unspeakable happened. Just one week after discovering my pregnancy, we walked through the valley of the shadow of death. I miscarried our little one, after our child grew only five weeks inside my womb.

As I typed the word miscarriage, the "mis" part tried to choke me with blame again. It's as if I was being accused of not carrying my child properly.

At the time of our loss, Mackey and I grieved hard. But we knew full well that God is the giver and taker of life and trusted His unknown plan. We knew our child now dwelled in His presence, rather than in ours, and that provided a sense of crazy peace when our circumstances made no sense.

Prior to losing our baby, Mac and I had already begun to ask God to reveal this child's name to us. From the moment He put the last beautiful body part of our child in place inside me, God had already selected the name of our precious infant. After our loss, in my spirit I knew that knowing his or her name would provide the beginning of some degree of closure for my heart. So Mackey and I prayed and waited on God, fully expecting an answer from Him.

Just a few weeks later, I received a phone call from a friend, Beverly. She suggested we take our five-year-olds to get their birthday pictures made. She wanted to take advantage of a pricing special offered by a photographer's studio near us. They mailed a coupon annually for each child in the household to get a free 8x10 for their birthday. I told Bev I needed to search for my coupon, and I'd call her back later.

I found the coupon. However, I discovered something on the piece of paper that surprised me—further evidence of God's personalized love and work in my life. The Portrait coupon did not have my five-year-old's name, but *David* was written on it instead. I took a second to recapture the breath that caught in my throat. This was one of the names that appeared on both mine and Mackey's baby name lists for boys.

I first called my husband, telling him through my messy cry how God had again showered us with His love, shown through answered prayer. Then I called Beverly, attempting to tell my friend what God had just done. But every awestruck word sounded jumbled in my effort to spit out the details of this miraculous name reveal. Finally, I managed to speak enough coherent sentences for my friend to figure out what I was telling her. Then she rejoiced with me, and we made plans to schedule the photo sessions for our little ones.

So often we withhold requests from God. We either fear our ask is too big or too small, or that there is something wrong with what we want Him to reveal. But God does not withhold the mysteries of the kingdom to those who ask. Jeremiah 33:3 says, "Call to Me and I will answer you, and I will tell you great and mighty things, which you do not know." Let that soak into your soul for just a moment . . . the All-Knowing God, Maker, and Keeper of all mysteries, will tell you things you do not know, great and mighty things, if you will only ask. I have experienced this more than once—by daring to believe. And that faith keeps me in crazy peace, no matter what I face.

When Mackey and I asked God to reveal the name of our waiting-in-Heaven child, our Father answered. Having confidence that our little David is safe in God's care, already glorifying the Father, brings me indescribable peace. God is absolutely the Almighty, and yet He is my closest friend. I can confide in Him, and He confides in me. Because His love and mercies never end, I'll tell the world all about what He has done, and is doing, until I am out of breath.

What about you? Do you have a need as tremendous and grief-filled as I did? It doesn't matter how much time has passed, God has not forgotten the concerns of your heart. He is the Alpha and the Omega, the beginning and the end. He is Almighty God, the Holy One, beyond all limitations of time. Most importantly, He cares for you and is close to the brokenhearted. Just pour your heart out to Him as you wait for His answer in His perfect timing. May He comfort your heart as He did mine, and may He cause any anxiety to disappear—no matter what its source or how much your faith seems to zigzag.

Opening Our Eyes

1. Are there requests you want to make of God but have held back? When you ask something of God, do you exercise faith by thanking Him in your prayers, prior to seeing or hearing the answers? *"So I say to you, ask, and it will be given to you; seek, and you will find; knock, and it will be opened to you. For everyone who asks receives, and the one who seeks finds, and to the one who knocks, it will be opened"* (Luke 11:9–10).

2. Have you or someone close to you ever lost a child? Do you, or they, anticipate a day of reunification in Heaven, where your tears will be dried, your sorrow taken away, and your hugs never ending? *Your eyes have seen my formless substance; And in Your book were written All the days that were ordained for me, When as yet there was not one of them* (Psalm 139:16).

CHAPTER TWENTY-FIVE

Zigzagging the Parking Lot

I'm so glad that God, as my dearest friend and greatest ally, never sleeps. Instead, He's a sentinel, standing guard, with His eye forever upon me—even when I find myself teetering on the edge of a mental disaster.

It happened so easily. I slipped into a routine of busying myself, living in my own strength without consulting God about my decisions. Obviously, I laid aside the power of prayer. I had unknowingly morphed into a spiritually weakened form of myself. I certainly was not casting my cares upon God, and that's where the danger began.

The enemy of our souls, Satan, has a mission—to prey upon wandering sheep. I had allowed myself to become his next possible candidate. My busyness made me so accessible that he handed me right over to one of his lesser minions. Might I introduce you to Mr. Anxiety?

Maybe you've met him before. Mr. Anxiety creeps around, lurking in doubting shadows when we start living independently from God. Mr. Anxiety's purposeful plan is to create destructive chaos in our lives. He waits for just the right moment to pounce. I first met him in a parking lot filled with vehicles of many colors, makes, and models.

The sizzling temperatures soared over 100 degrees, close to a Mississippi record. It was so hot you could have fried bacon on the hood of my car. The sweltering temps also happened to arrive during the season of my life when I had a private, hormone-fueled "personal heating system" roaring at full capacity. Menopause is not a time of high fun or fashion. Sweating isn't what a lady does in the South, but this lady had more going on than a mere glistening.

Strangely enough, I have always enjoyed challenging myself with insane schedules, even when the odds and the clock were both against me. Why? I do not know. But the pressure exhilarates me. That day, I had planned with my usual modus operandi—I would hurry to shop, drive my groceries home, and return to meet a friend, all in one hour.

Exiting a favorite store, the electric doors swished behind me. I headed to where I remembered parking my van, but Mr. Anxiety followed close behind. My grocery buggy was filled with perishables, chocolates, and frozen items, all potentially disastrous choices for a July shopping list. I calculated about how quickly it would take the ice cream to melt in the steamy heat before I arrived home, and my confidence began to fizzle.

I took a deep breath and reminded myself that I could overcome the odds. But within a few minutes, as I steered that buggy up and down the parking lot, I realized I'd lost my van. I had no idea where I'd parked.

As the asphalt grew hotter, and my stress level rose, I stepped up my pace which in turn raised my grocery cart speedometer. The faster I walked, however, the faster my confidence slipped away. The van was nowhere in sight. I could feel Mr. Anxiety now breathing on my neck.

Then a profound revelation struck me. I told myself, *No worries. I needn't look for the van because I didn't drive it today. I brought Mackey's car.* It didn't take long for my hopes to shrivel in the Mississippi summer sun though, my search started back at square one.

I pushed the buggy up and down the same meandering path, careening up and down, zigzagging rows of vehicles. Only this time, I searched for my husband's black Town Car. I soon realized it, too, was nowhere to be found.

Realizing I couldn't recognize either my van or Mackey's Town Car in the crowded lot, my stress levels soared to new heights. No more feigning lady-like protocols, this was no genteel matter. I traded in my Southern glistening glow for an off the charts, full-out, pouring-down-the-back-and-front river of sweat. All command of my senses headed to a screeching halt. I stood in the middle of that parking lot, a.k.a. frying pan, and mentally melted. Oddly, I still managed to restrain the tears waiting for permission to fall.

This is where prayer should've been inserted, but it was not. Instead, I dug down within myself, searching for extra strength, while in my own efforts I attempted to keep Mr. Anxiety's best friend, Ms. Panic at bay. He really didn't need her help though because he was doing a fine job on me all by himself. My blood pressure revved to extremes, my stomach churned with large doses of acid, and my breathing came in stressed fits and spurts. My confidence plummeted as I mentally beat myself up.

Who loses a whole vehicle?

How could you be so stupid?

Why didn't you pay more attention when you parked?

I'm pretty sure that both Mr. Anxiety and Ms. Panic were giggling as I slipped into this vortex of out-of-controlness. (Yes, I made that word up.) I did my best to ward off all images of men in white coats coming to get me and carry me away to some room with cushion buffered walls. Was this the twilight zone? For a couple of minutes, I questioned how I'd even managed to get to the shopping center.

Knowing I needed to get a grip, I concentrated on slowing my intake of air and deepening my breathing. *Think.* I demanded of myself. *Retrace your morning. If you didn't drive the van, and you didn't bring Mackey's Town car either, how did you get here?* Then it dawned on me.

That morning I had chosen to drive our small sedan, which typically sat unused in our driveway. Though I rarely gave it a glance, this was the day I decided to take the poor pitiful thing out for a ride, giving it a workout to the super center. Of course, by the time of my epiphany, Mr. Anxiety and Ms. Panic had made themselves quite visible in me. Quite a crowd had gathered to offer assistance to the crazy lady.

I explained the reason for my alarm, telling the group I was searching for my unknown vehicle. These kind souls patiently offered to help—they just needed some crucial information.

"What color is it?" a woman asked.

"I don't remember," I said.

"What kind of car is it?" a man asked.

"I don't know that either," I responded.

Not sure exactly what I was looking for, I started pushing my buggy again, on the hunt for a vehicle I knew only as a small sedan. A few folks meandered away from me, probably frustrated with my inability to give even the tiniest bit of detail, but most of the crowd stuck it out. They accompanied me for a third try as I searched for my car up and down the rows, while they continued to ask essential questions.

"Is it a two-tone or solid color?" a guy asked.

I answered him with a blank stare. I was way out of my element. My knowledge of cars started and ended with where to insert the key and the gasoline hose. I spotted the side glances some of my helpers exchanged.

"Does it have two doors or four?" a woman asked.

My heart leapt inside my chest. "I know, it's a four-door sedan," I said with absolute conviction. "It's an older car," I added. "But I don't know how old. There's no key fob to blink or honk. There is a number pad on the door, though. And I do remember the code," I said proudly.

This was a great clue, but I could tell by the looks on their faces there weren't many believers left among the search crew. The bottom line was that although they were clueless as to the make, model, color, or age of my mystery car, they at least now knew to look for a number pad.

With the help of the resolute few long-suffering friends now sticking it out with me, I continued to zigzag the aisles. By then I finally remembered to pray. Sadly, what should have been my first action was my last. Thankfully, God doesn't hold our delays against us, He's just happy when we realize we've forgotten to include Him in our needs and correct it.

By this time, though a handful of people had drifted off, my entourage of friendly car-hunters began to grow. I don't doubt that some joined the crowd merely to see if I would be escorted to the police station or if an ambulance would show up to carry me off. I was one hot mess—both literally and metaphorically.

Having zigzagged back to the beginning of my quest, something caught my eye. I shouted, "I found it!" I'd spotted the sedan in the first row where I'd previously hunted for my van. I probably overlooked it the first two times I'd hunted there because I was searching for a mini-van or a black Town Car instead of a blue sedan.

Quickly, I was surrounded by cheering people.

"Awesome," one person said.

"Congratulations," added another.

"See, patience pays off," someone else told me.

I entered the code in the pin pad and thanked my fan club as I quickly loaded the melting groceries in the back seat. Then I drove home to unpack and put away the semi-frozen foods and other perishables. However, though I was in a rush, I took a moment to note the shade, make, and model of my previously unknown vehicle. It was a light blue Ford Taurus—something I would never forget again.

Later I reflected on the events of the day. *Thank goodness God always knows exactly where I am and where my things are.* I thought, *But why didn't I turn to Him first? His peace could've easily protected me from Mr. Anxiety and his comrade, Ms. Panic. They are my enemies, but they hold no power in comparison to God. Neither they nor their master, Satan, are matches for the Lord God of Hosts.* Instantly my crazy peace was restored.

Still I can't help wondering, what if I had prayed sooner? I could've asked God for the row and vehicle type earlier that day. A prayer of faith could've saved me from the entire fiasco, and I could've gotten my groceries home before the melting had begun. How could I have forgotten that the Creator of all, dwelling inside of me, doesn't mind mundane requests? Even parking dilemmas are not beyond His interest or His reach. He is omniscient and cares about every detail of life, the serious and the ridiculous. He's never too busy to listen or rescue, as would any good Father.

I still wonder if those kind car-hunters ever recall the escapade of the frazzled lady and her mystery car. Can't I just blame it all on the heat?

I find that when I call on God early instead of later, not only do I experience crazy peace during heated moments, but it also helps keep Mr. Anxiety and Ms. Panic at bay. My guess is that they're assigned Southern parking lots, because they like high temps. And they're assigned to widows, because they appear to be easy targets. But God is always full of surprises.

Opening Our Eyes

1. Have you ever forgotten to pray, only to discover that the moment you did, your answer came? Do you ask God to tell you which way to go on a daily basis? Why or why not? *I will instruct you and teach you in the way which you should go. I will advise you with My eye upon you* (Psalm 32:8).

2. How has praying and/or Bible reading diffused anxiety and a sense of panic for you? Have you ever considered how much God cares about the emotions you carry, and His willingness to take your burdens away? *I cared for you in the wilderness, In the land of drought* (Hosea 13:5).

CHAPTER TWENTY-SIX

Mailbox Reformation

Who knew that knocking down mailboxes would bring some entertainment to the attacked? And who knew that a mailbox and post cost $391 to replace? After learning that little detail, I had a serious discussion with The One who holds my heart, hand, and checkbook.

As a newly widowed woman, I experienced attacks on my emotions, especially on my once confident state of mind. After each episode, I reminded myself that although I had a loving man for forty-two years of marriage, I was husbandless and God was now my husband, taking care of me. That knowledge was magnified when I faced yet another fiasco after Mackey passed.

It was a Sunday morning, and I started backing out of the driveway on my way to church. I glanced toward the edge of my street, where my mailbox lay on the ground. However, not only was the box broken, but one half of the metal post, decorated with metal filigree, was also on the ground.

I immediately figured it was probably a prank perpetrated by some bored teens out on a nightly rampage of senseless mischief. Or maybe my mailbox was victimized by a young lad who was "double-dog-dared" to attack it. But as I inspected my neighbors' boxes on the left and then to those on my right, I realized that theirs were all intact. Mine was the sole receptor of destruction.

Having recently walked through the darkest days of my life, I cried out. "Why God? Why me? I can't take much more. This is so unfair."

I felt more vulnerable than ever before in my new state of widowhood. I already had an overwhelming list of things to tend to as the newly designated sole homeowner. Things that had never broken before were forcing me to learn a myriad of new skills. None of these challenges held the least bit of interest, beyond their functioning state. I stared down the lame mailbox for several seconds and decided there was nothing I could do until after Sunday services. So I drove off, vowing to deal with it later.

Once I returned from church, I contacted my homeowner's association, asking for information on how to get a replacement mailbox that fit our neighborhood criteria. I gulped when the man on the phone told me the requirements.

"It will cost $126 for the box, $65 for the numbers, and $200 for the post," he said.

It didn't take much time for me to do the math in my head. "Seriously?"

After I hung up, I discussed the matter with God. "Okay, I dedicated everything I own to You, so if this is how You want me to use *Your* money, then so be it. I will." I continued praying. "Please give me peace and wisdom about what to do next."

Then suddenly, I knew what to do. I sent out a prayer request to my support system of faithful friends. Immediately three men in my church's small group said they could fix my mailbox. It was as if they were in a race for the blessing of helping out a needy and very frustrated widow.

Feeling relieved and deeply grateful, I told the group that whoever came over to repair my mailbox first was the winner. It took no time for someone to take me up on the challenge.

The very next day, the winning helper, Terry, showed up, despite severely cold weather. He jumped right in and went to work, starting by digging up the bottom half of the wrought iron post. In a matter of hours, he had hauled it away, along with the badly dented mailbox. He promised to return the next weekend to complete the job.

In the interim, I set up an old mailbox and labeled it with my address. My temporary collection receptacle worked just fine for my mail carrier.

A week later, Terry returned. I watched him as he dug a deeper hole and placed the newly soldered and painted post into it. Next, he poured some fresh concrete around the post and patted it until it was smooth and firmly set upright in the ground. He then added the box on top.

As I watched him from inside my window, emotions consumed me and turned into tears that dripped off my face. To me, Terry's actions symbolized the care of God, as the husband to my husbandless self. It was as if Jesus Himself was repairing my mailbox. But that wasn't my only realization, triggered by the scene before me.

While Terry labored. I poured forth my frustrated anger, speaking out loud to the enemy, Satan. I shouted my truths, as God's spiritual wife.

"You CANNOT take me down!"

"I am NOT alone!"

"My Jesus is stronger than you!"

"I refuse to let you steal my joy!"

"Jesus already won this victory!"

"You lose!"

After I finished pouring my soul out, a precious thought flooded my mind. If my mailbox hadn't been destroyed, I would have missed out on an opportunity to witness God at work through the body of Christ. My heart and my home were instantly filled with crazy peace. This is what I learned then and know today.

I am able to stand upright against all attacks because my foundation, Jesus Christ, is the Cornerstone. He is strong like that set concrete, holding me firmly in place. Because I am held safely in Christ, I stand confidently. God is my forever husband, watching over me and leading me with His wisdom. Because I am His . . .

I am NOT vulnerable.

I am NOT alone.

I am NOT defeated.

I AM more than a conqueror.

I AM an overcomer in Christ Jesus!

Today these are the truths I speak whenever the enemy comes lurking around, seeking to destroy. I can remind him who is in charge. It is not uncommon for me to stand in the middle of my room and proclaim, "You can rest assured, you devil you, this woman will not be torn down. The God I serve has already won the battle, and He is not only my warrior, He is my husband."

Now every day I check my box for mail, I am reminded that I am held firmly—God keeps me strong. This gives me the resolve not to lose my joy over something silly, like a downed piece of metal. Sometimes it takes a trial to give you a fresh revelation of the reality of God's Word. And that's a permanent blessing.

Opening Our Eyes

1. When has God taken a difficult circumstance and created something beautiful out of it for you? What is the greatest, most amazing, outrageous thing God has ever done to show you His love and care? *Now to Him who is able to do far more abundantly beyond all that we ask or think, according to the power that works within us* (Ephesians 3:20).

2. Have you witnessed, or have you ever been a part of, an answered prayer for someone else? How many of the negatives in your life ended up with a surprisingly positive outcome? *As for you, you meant evil against me, but God meant it for good in order to bring about this present result, to keep many people alive* (Genesis 50:20).

CHAPTER TWENTY-SEVEN

Permanently Temporary or Temporarily Permanent

A *rolling stone gathers no moss.* This proverb is credited to Publilius Syrus[2]. In his *Sententiae* he stated, "People who are always moving, with no roots in one place or another, avoid responsibilities and cares." But in the twenty-first century, the saying carries more of a connotation, meaning someone who stays on the move and gets things done.

This could indeed be said of my life, probably by my mama. She used to complain that I messed up her address book. My many moves caused her to erase my address and phone number way too many times—twenty to be exact.

It was my husband's job that led, or dragged me kicking, through each move to a new living location. We never knew when, or if, a change of address was really coming.

2 https://en.wikipedia.org/wiki/A_rolling_stone_gathers_no_moss

There were a couple of times when Mackey's company informed us that we'd be transferred within the week, and we believed them. Friends and neighbors hosted going-away parties for us, complete with gifts, tears, and all, and no moving trucks showed up. After some time passed when that happened, I would spot one of those friends around town, and feel as though I should ask if they wanted their gift back. How embarrassing was that?

This constant, not-really-knowing-when-we-were-moving spurred our saying, "When the moving truck drives up, that's when we're moving." In our world, we had no choice but to adapt.

There were plenty of replanting opportunities in the earlier years of my marriage to Mackey. This is the lifestyle of a nuclear field engineer. Little did I know any of this when I stood at the altar and said, "I do." But I committed to go with my honey everywhere he went. I had to replant myself into many a small, unknown town because they just don't build nuclear plants in large cities. Very shortly into our state of wedded bliss, God dropped a spoken word in my spirit. He told me to "live temporarily permanent and not permanently temporary."

Read that last sentence above again. Slowly. Then let it sink in.

This wisdom truly impacted me, bringing me crazy peace through tumultuous times. It kept me from living for tomorrow, wasting away the "today" of every move. Instead, I made the most of every moment surrounding me, and enjoyed a lot more years, as a result. I learned to live to the fullest, meet plenty of friends, get to know my neighbors, sign up for library cards, find shortcuts when driving, explore and invest in each city, and make the most of every minute I had there. I chose the attitude "This is a necessary part of life," even if it meant we would again fill out those dreaded "forward my mail" cards, two months later.

As I look back, I can definitely say that the greatest challenge to my contented state of mind was living in six states during my first pregnancy. That proved a bit much, even for my determinedly positive mindset. Where would we be in my ninth month? Who would deliver our baby? Of course, God was the only one who knew those plans. And He faithfully carried us through all of the unknowns during those many relocations.

Forty-two years of marriage, twenty change-of-address cards, and four children later, I can look back and see the handiwork of God. He not only helped me survive, but He helped my body, spirit, and mind flourish and thrive. The length of my Christmas card list provides evidence of the friends in every city we called home. Throughout the south and northeastern U.S. I was blessed to experience crazy peace as I learned to live temporarily permanent.

For a girl who had never ventured north of Shreveport, Louisiana, our extremely nomadic life proved a fantastic feat. Prior to marrying Mac, I had lived life in the "permanently permanent" mode, never traveling far from home or extended family. God knew that my becoming the wife of a nuclear field engineer would exponentially expand my limited horizon. He had bigger plans for me.

With each move, I again had to tear myself away from good friends I'd found. It felt excruciating to pull up roots and transfer away from them. But with each new move, God always had more friends waiting for me, wherever we went. I didn't lose relationships, I gained them.

During one season of our marriage, we actually remained in one place for twelve years without a change of address. I had developed some deep-rooted friendships, and they were tightly entangled in my heartstrings. So when the dreaded news finally came that we were to move, I questioned God. I did everything possible to procrastinate against the preparations for another tear-away event, until during my prayer time I felt God speak precious words of comfort to me.

"You know the friends you love here? It's Me in them."

The thought lessened the sting I was feeling, at least a little.

"You know the church you love here? It's Me in there as well."

I pondered that truth too.

"You know the homeschool group you love here? It's Me in them. I'm going with you, and you will see me in the people you meet in your new location, as much as you've seen me in the people here."

I realized I could invest myself anywhere God was drawing us to. My husband's company may have thought they were in control of where we were going, but my Father had those plans fully orchestrated in advance. I voiced my acceptance. "Okay then, I'm all in, Jesus. Now, where exactly is my new city located on the map?"

For all of us, every act of faith we demonstrate is an intimate act of love shown to God. From which job we take, to house-hunting, to visiting churches, to deciding which organizations to affiliate with, to meeting and making new friends, these are all parts of His glorious plans for our lives. Accepting and embracing His greater good proves our commitment to Him.

Although God allows us free will to choose for or against His best plans, I have learned to wait on His Spirit to lead and direct for the greatest outcomes. There is no fear for tomorrow or where we will end up because His love is perfect. God will never leave or forsake us. I can attest to His loving protection because I have seen His excellent ways proven right for my family and me, time and time again.

Are you living temporarily permanent, making the most of your time in your replanted position? Or are you grumbling and complaining, making yourself and those around you miserable, while you subsist with a permanently temporary mindset? Relying on God makes life one big, exciting challenge as we watch Him enfold His lovingkindness, surrounding us. Our Father absolutely knows what is best for our lives.

Looking back, I can say, "It's been a great ride, God! Thank You for enriching my life with the many gifts of people and experiences throughout the years and teaching me contentment in all circumstances. There's no better gift than Your hand on my life." This will be my prayer until the finish.

Opening Our Eyes

1. When you are faced with a situation that scares or frustrates you, do you trust God and choose a higher mindset, or do you grumble and complain? How do you fix your focus on the positives God calls us to? *Finally, brothers and sisters, whatever is true, whatever is honorable, whatever is right, whatever is pure, whatever is lovely, whatever is commendable, if there is any excellence and if anything worthy of praise, think about these things* (Philippians 4:8).

2. What are the most challenging aspects of the fruit of God's Spirit for you to live out? How do you return God's goodness for all He does for you? *But the fruit of the Spirit is love, joy, peace, patience, kindness, goodness, faithfulness, gentleness, self-control; against such things there is no law* (Galatians 5:22–23).

CHAPTER TWENTY-EIGHT

Finishing Well

H ave you ever faced a situation that should have terrified you, only to feel surrounded by a strange sense of unexplainable calm? It happened to me through a personal "reset."

My healthcare team found two suspicious spots that changed my life instantly. Naturally this led to more appointments, filling my calendar from November to July—as of this writing.

I faced the new adventure with a most unusual sense of serenity—even I didn't understand it. That crazy peace carried me from my unwanted October surprise in Mississippi, when I went for my first medical visit, into January, when I saw a Texas specialist for a second opinion. I felt confident God *could* provide a welcome alternative to my initial diagnosis of stage four gallbladder cancer. My question was, *would* He? And if He chose not to give me an immediate miracle, would my crazy peace hold out? How would my family deal with a "worst case scenario?"

I spent the day and night prior to my Texas appointment in a waiting bubble, which on the outside, looked as if nothing was new. Inside my body though, cells were changing. The second opinion verified the first. I would get the answers to my questions.

My stage four gallbladder cancer required me to start chemo right away, but crazy peace again surrounded me in the few precious days before beginning. I even managed to edit a few stories, focusing on doing the next right thing versus dwelling on an unknown future I could neither predict or change.

But as serene as I felt about myself, I did not like seeing what cancer did to my kids. The diagnosis blasted the lives of my four children and their spouses. Not only were they concerned about my well-being, but as they helped navigate the unknown-to-us-world of chemo and whatever it might bring, their lives were upended with new time restraints and schedules. I watched my children become research experts, learning the correct pronunciations of vocabulary terms none of us wanted to know. Ultimately my disease changed all of our lives.

But early on, I was reminded that God had a call on my life, one that even the "c" word couldn't destroy. I remained committed to telling as many people as possible about Christ's bloodshed for them and the salvation awaiting their one decision to accept His offer of absolute forgiveness and unconditional love. But even in my resolve, a couple of questions plagued me and prompted me to mentally ask God:

Will they believe You?
Will they receive You?

Ultimately I understood it is not for me to know another person's eternal outcome, but it is simply for me to spread the love of God wherever I have opportunity. My health situation offered a bright light of possibility—I would carry the message and example of Christ's offered acceptance into every medical office and examination room possible.

The first time I sat in the infusion chair, it took a bit for me to relax. But I soon adapted to the drips, occasional beeps, and conversations around me. Once I became accustomed to my surroundings, a mix of thoughts crowded my mind. I wondered, *Will the fear of losing their only living parent draw my children to face their own aging process? I hope going through this stirs their faith to even greater heights. I know they each believe in Jesus Christ as their Savior, but will the crazy peace I'm blessed with sustain them throughout this difficult time? And will they see new opportunities to share God's message of hope because of my cancer journey?*

But there was little time to concentrate on my concerns. One more crisis was coming. One that would impact us worldwide.

The Covid-19 challenge of 2020 automatically stripped away much of the fluff of life and complacent activities we once thought were necessary. For me, I missed ministering to widows and providing hospitality to international dancers, but there was a side benefit. Covid-19 cleared all the pages of my calendar and allowed me to focus even more on my health and writing.

Still, I attempted to create a daily purpose in my life. I continued participating in Bible study but took the time to really analyze my motives as much as my efforts. I asked myself a series of questions. *Am I doing this study just to be busy and finish the lesson so I can say that I completed the assignment? Is reading the Bible drawing me into a closer relationship with Jesus, or has it become a mere habit? (I'm afraid I know that answer.)*

The more I reflected, the more I was drawn to get alone with God and talk to Him out loud. My prayers soon became very personal, where I spilled out my feelings, desires, and hopes. I took everything to Him because He was always accessible and always safe. No emotion or thought was off limits—I was speaking boldly, like I never had before.

"Lord, before rescuing me from this physical life and bringing me to Paradise, where I will get to be by Your side forever, please help me put my hand to what You want me to do. My mind cannot even comprehend everything You've allowed me to see and experience, much less what's left to finish.

"And help me to act intentionally in every tiny or large daily event. Since 1977, You've opened my eyes through the reading of Your Word, the Bible, so I know Your heart to rescue souls. Thank You for giving me a desire to share in that task. Who are they, Lord?

"Is it the delivery person who brings my groceries or prescriptions, now that Covid has temporarily ended my shopping trips? Is it the person on the other end of the phone, helping me figure out how to complete yet another pile of paperwork? Is it the person on social media, who needs a break by seeing some lightness amidst all those dark posts? Is it a doctor, a nurse, a receptionist, or a shuttle driver? Please put me in the path of those You want me to influence, and open my eyes, so I do not miss a single opportunity to reflect Your love."

As I write this, I am still in treatment for cancer. I have no idea what my end outcome will be or how many days God has yet numbered for me on this planet. But until I am called home to heaven, I am willing to fight for more time on earth. I am committed to filtering out the unimportant so I can make time for the eternally crucial. Souls are at stake!

Cancer has shown me my limitations of time and strength, so I must make wise decisions as to how to utilize each grain of sand within the hourglass I have left. I'm no longer interested in wasting time on earth. Of course, none of us knows the number of our days, but I might meet Jesus, face to face, much sooner than I was thinking.

Recently, my siblings began the task of helping me filter out the unnecessary within my home. It was fun but exhausting, going through decades of mementos, souvenirs, and communications with loved ones. Some of the emotions triggered by my accumulated possessions caught me off-guard. But I've also become weary from making decisions, and even more so, from spending time to accomplish the seemingly endless tasks required to prepare me for a possible flight to eternity. And yet, that crazy peace presides.

As I consider my family, neighbors, and friends, I know each one will reach a point where they must face their own mortality head-on, just as they are now watching me face mine. You, dear reader, will one day find yourself in a similar place. When that time comes, I pray you are equally filled with the same kind of crazy peace that I am.

The thought of remaining alive on earth, where I can share, encourage, and hopefully help draw others to the one real, lasting, and trustworthy relationship they can count on, through belief in Jesus Christ, infuses me with supernatural energy. But the thought of being absent from my body and being with Him, makes me hunger for my true home.

Contemplating my own survival or death, I've written this book with others in mind. Whether I still have breath in my body as you read these words, or whether I'm ecstatically enjoying my eternity, this is my ultimate prayer. My final word to you, my reading friend, is the enduring hope that a similar desire beats within your own heart.

Lord, I want time to wrap things up. I want to leave my messages of You in an orderly fashion, so others can digest and understand just how amazing You are and how very much You love them. I want to leave a lasting word that will continue to serve You once I'm done here on earth.

May Your crazy peace exude onto the who-so-evers of life who come after me. Use my words, Lord— they're all I have left. Anoint this book and spread it far and wide, so that many others can learn just how BIG You are and yet how close You yearn for them to be to You. Open their eyes to see You in their everyday events. May they finish well for Your glory!

I love You, Lord, and I am NOT afraid. Please comfort my children and other loved ones. I know the pain of loss, but I also stand confident that I will pass from this life into Your waiting arms!

While I wait to see You with real eyes, I know You are closer than I could ever imagine in this moment. A part of me is ready to be with You but help me to fight harder if it will better serve You for me to stay here a little longer. The assurance of Your presence in body or in spirit is my Crazy Peace. And for that I am thankful. Your will be done, in Jesus' Name.

Opening Our Eyes

1. When you imagine crossing into eternity, what about your time on earth matters most? Have you considered how your life might win souls for Jesus Christ? *The fruit of the righteous is a tree of life, And the one who is wise gains souls* (Proverbs 11:30).

2. How can you testify to the evidence of God's powerful hand at work in your life? What do you need to do to finish the course set before you? *But I do not consider my life of any account as dear to myself, so that I may finish my course and the ministry which I received from the Lord Jesus, to testify solemnly of the gospel of God's grace* (Acts 20:24).

What to Leave Behind?

Knowing that my earthen treasures will be left behind, counted, distributed, and given away to strangers, the most important treasure I want to leave intact is my legacy of faith. Although I have cherished those things left to me from past generations, I sense that my children have never quite caught hold of the same vision or feeling of joy over these items as I have felt. I am still striving to accept this fact.

I worked on a cross-stitched piece years ago which still proudly claims a slot of real estate on my wall. It reads: *There are two special gifts we should give our children; one is roots and the other is wings.*

Mother Theresa must have wholeheartedly agreed with this, because she is quoted as saying, "You will teach them to fly, but they will not fly your flight. You will teach them to dream, but they will not dream your dream. You will teach them to live, but they will not live your life. Nevertheless, in every flight, in every dream, in every life, the print of the way you taught them will remain."

It takes far less effort to care for and pass down my favored physical possessions than to impart my spiritual treasures and values. Yes, that antique coat of mine will cause some laughter after I'm gone, just as some of my personal values have caused a few chuckles, even those rooted in the Word of God. But they both provide a form of protection. The former provides temporary warmth when I'm cold, and the latter will serve as a long-term defense for my soul.

The truth is that evil forces surround us all. Our cell phones and televisions spill out various disasters, both natural and man-derived, before our eyes every day. Yet, we carry on in oblivion, blind to the movements in the spiritual realm. Our God is on constant sentinel watch, daily and throughout our nights, casting down evil destructive forces, unbeknownst to us.

Sometimes I forget and slip into daily living a bit flippantly, as if I am above the dangers of everyday events in my own feeble strength. Yet, I can recall any number of stories whereby God's intervention has saved me, and immediately my faith is strengthened. God always shows up and He loves to show out.

Before I depart from this earth, my temporary home, I want to intentionally count and distribute some of the faith stories of God's gracious touch on my life. For sure, I want to leave a priceless legacy of my spiritual possession to my children and grandchildren, but I also want to leave a portion to you and yours.

Through this book, I've introduced you to "El Roi, the God who sees," and shared my confidence about His loving care. He hovers over His beloved children with the passion and protection of a mama eagle watching over her young. If you allow Him, He will fight for you with the same inexhaustible power as He has shown me.

I urge you to join me in renewed awareness of God working in your everyday events, and then credit Him with His supernatural touches on your life. By living intentionally, and in expectation of His actions, you too will find evidence of God's loving fingerprints marking your every move.

But whenever you need a fresh reminder, as I sometimes do, pick this book back up and immerse yourself in a testimony of His lavish love and protection, remembering what He's done within these pages. What He's done for me, He can also do for you.

Crazy peace comes from the confidence we gain in trusting God, knowing that we all can leave behind a legacy of hope, even if at times, it looks too silly to believe!

Acknowledgements

This book would not be possible without the support and encouragement of my family, friends, and most of all, the call from my Heavenly Father.

Mackey, you were my greatest encourager, even when my faith walk seemed to teeter on the laughable. You were my honey and my Smack-a-Jack, and one of my greatest gifts from God. You always encouraged me to write and paint, you were the wind beneath my wings, no matter what I had up my sleeve or in my brain to do. Our big God who still speaks today, spoke to me through you, as you confirmed His callings. I still struggle to do life without you—and look forward to our reunion in Heaven.

Doug, Scott, Micah, and Bethany, thank you for supporting your mom. Your love has carried me while I journeyed through cancer and did the impossible to write this book. May His Word sustain and encourage you to walk boldly with God.

Doug, a.k.a. Dougie Bug, your antics as my number one son have given me much more to write about than this book can contain. Your constant inquiring mind has inspired me, yet I can't possibly keep up with some of your brilliant thinking. You figure out the world's problems, and I'll just write.

Scott, my surprise boy, took us to the ER more times than we thought possible. I think we kept Band-Aid in business because of you. Today your service as a captain in the Air Force protects our family and our nation, and I couldn't be prouder. It is deeply appreciated. Sorry I kept you from being a major league pitcher.

Micah, my sweetie girl, finally a little bit of pinkness arrived when you joined our world. You are my favorite CPA and always will be. Thank you for your organizational giftings that created my chemo bags and medication spreadsheets. You help keep your mom going.

Bethany, my B, who led us all down the path of dance as you worked toward becoming a professional ballerina. You used your feet and your faith, to serve the Lord around the world. You inspire me and so many others.

To my four grands, Liora, Connor, Charis, and Cate, from the day I met each of you, I have loved you. You absolutely light up my life. I am so blessed to be your Nana.

To my sisters, Diane and Patty, the queens of decluttering, thanks for ever reminding me that "we spend half of our lives collecting things and the other half trying to give it away." You have supported me through my cancer journey. You lift my spirits and make me laugh—you also give me some great writing fodder at times.

Ann Glover, you will always be an inspiration to me for asking me that most important question, "Are you a Christian?" My list of answers was extensive, but none were good enough. You let me know that only through accepting a personal relationship with Jesus by confessing my sins and allowing Him to cover them with His blood, could I be saved and changed. Thank You for the prayer that brought me into the throne room of grace for eternity. Through these forty-four years as a friend, you have patiently answered my myriad of questions. Your gentle yet bold spirit has been a shining light.

Jayne Kier, thank you for admitting you are the other half of my brain and being my cohort in crimes of craziness. I can't imagine what my life would have been like without you.

Robin Tate, I appreciate you for serving as my memory of all things past. Your recall of the most minute details makes my recollections richer. You wisely reminded me to hold on to my crazy peace which God spoke to my heart—especially when others don't understand it. It's His word to me.

Anita Brooks, it would have been impossible to get these words on paper without you. Thank you for taking my stories and making them better with your excellent writing and editing skills, but more so, I appreciate your patience. You clearly put the flesh on my bony stories. I've learned so much from your painting the scenes of my life.

Carol McLeod, author of thirteen books and cheerleader extraordinaire, your initial encouragement to take the big step and get my stories off the laptop and into others' hands made this book possible. Thank you for leading me to Suzanne Kuhn and Anita Brooks of Brookstone Publishing Group. Meeting you through a North Carolina homeschooling co-op was certainly for such a time as this.

Suzanne Kuhn, thank you for your expertise in all things book publishing, and for bringing together an amazing team of professionals. Brookstone Publishing Group gave me a lot of *Crazy Peace* through the crazy writing and publication process.

My Jesus, Lord and Savior, Your plan for my life has been filled with many highs and lows. But I trust it will always bring You glory. My family took me to church and taught me about Your birth, death, and resurrection, but until the scales were taken off my eyes later in life, I didn't understand that You did that for me. Personally! Thank You for the way You adore me, as You do all of Your beloved children.

Jesus, I am so grateful You taught me to rest in Your truth and provision, expressed in Hebrews 9:22, "without the shedding of blood there is no forgiveness of sins." Thank You for shedding Your blood for me, but for also doing so for every person You draw to read these words. Without Your call on my life, there would be no book, and certainly no crazy peace. I stand in awestruck amazement that You would use the least of these—me. I love You!

Linda Hurstell

Photo Credit: Christina Freeman

Linda Hurstell is a speaker, teacher, and writer, and she has even produced and directed a children's musical theater troupe. She wants others to know how they can enjoy an intimate relationship with God, for He is as close as a whispered prayer.

Linda was married for 42 years until she was recently widowed. She is the mother of four and is now called Nana by four. Her stories of faith are 100-percent true and yet riddled with a certain amount of ridiculousness, which explains her "crazy peace, crazy love, crazy strength from above," as a fellow cancer fighter once said.